Peak

Distric

Monsters

by

Alan Smith

Sketches by Alan Smith.

Maps by John N. Merrill.

Trail Crest Publications Ltd.

1994

Sandia Mountains
New Mexico. USA

TRAIL CREST PUBLICATIONS Ltd.,

Milne House,
Speedwell Mill,
Miller's Green,
Wirksworth,
Derbyshire
DE4 4BL

(0629) 826354
(0629) 826354

Edited, typeset, designed, paged, printed, marketed and distributed by John N. Merrill.

© Text, & sketches - Alan Smith1994.
© Maps - John N. Merrill 1994.

First Published - November 1994.

ISBN 1 874754 45 4

Please note - The maps in this guide are purely illustrative. You are encouraged to use the appropriate 1:25,000 O.S. map.

U.S.A. office - P.O. Box 124, Santa Rosa, New Mexico 88435 U.S.A.

Meticulous research has been undertaken to ensure that this publication is highly accurate at the time of going to press. The publishers, however, cannot be held responsible for alterations, errors or omissions, but they would welcome notification of such for future editions.

Typeset in - Palatino - bold, italic and plain 9pt and 18pt.

Printed and designed by - Footprint Press Ltd./John N. Merrill at Milne House, Speedwell Mill, Miller's Green, Wirksworth, Derbyshire. DE4 4BL.

Cover sketch "Dovedale Deadnead".
© Alan Smith,1994.

An all British product.

For my Mother and Father

CONTENTS

ABOUT THE AUTHOR

Born in 1948 and brought up in a working class home in Middlesbrough - Father was a lorry driver. In 1970 moved to Nottingham to train as a teacher and frequently visits the Peak District with his family, with school groups, or alone. Fascination for the countryside and wildlife began at an early age, on family outings to the North Yorkshire Moors.

His first book - "Working Out of Doors with Young People" (ISBN 185202 002 4) - based on his work as a teacher of Geography and Outdoor Education. A new edition of this book now titled - "Creative Outdoor Work with Young People" (ISBN 898924 25 2) is being published @ £9.95 by Russell House Publishing Ltd., Russell House, Lym Close, Lyme Regis, Dorset. DT7 3DE

Other books in preparation being published by Trail Crest Publications Ltd -

Book No. 2 - "Monsters of the North Yorkshire Moors."
Book No. 3 - "Lake District Monsters."

PREFACE

When we go out into the countryside, we subconsciously prepare ourselves to see the familiar species of wildlife that we know exist in a particular area. Our background knowledge, built up from childhood, through holidays, books and television, tells us what to expect. Each time we visit these places our perception is reinforced. Is it possible that we have been unwittingly conditioned to look only for the normal or acceptable life forms? This book is about things, known and unknown, that live in a very special area of the British Isles, a place surrounded by towns and cities, yet relatively unspoilt.

The Peak District of Derbyshire has a unique variety of landscape within its area. Windswept moorlands lie to the north, dramatic limestone valleys drain to the south, and precipitous gritstone edges guard the eastern and western boundaries. Below the surface of this region is a hidden world of caverns and subterranean passages.

Sharing these diverse habitats with the more well known fauna are a number of creatures, referred to in this book as the Peak District Monsters. These fascinating species co-exist in harmony with their surroundings. Visitors to the area often come quite close to the monsters without noticing them, or perhaps they prefer to 'turn a blind eye'.

The collective term 'monsters' may initially paint a picture in our imagination of terrifying beasts with unsavoury predatory habits, but this image is certainly not true of the Peak District Monsters. These, in the main, are shy intelligent creatures that have evolved and adapted their behaviour to suit their special surroundings. At times some may be mischievous and occasionally troublesome, yet none are malicious or cruel.

They have successfully survived in this popular area without interference from their human neighbours. Hopefully we will grow to understand and accept their strange habits.

*"As if obsessed by some great urgency, the Bog Bouncer shot across the Bleaklow plateau,
thoroughly enjoying its early morning romp."*

CHAPTER
1

THE BLEAKLOW BOG BOUNCER

The winter had been milder than usual up on Bleaklow hill. Only a trace of snow remained, and the surface was wet and boggy, even by Bleaklow's standards. A strong southwesterly wind was blowing over the moor, as daylight slowly appeared over the skyline. Dark clouds raced over the inhospitable uplands, almost touching the highest points.

Sheltered in a natural hollow amongst the gritstone tors, crouched the Bog Bouncer with arms folded and eye lids starting to open. The first dull light had touched its weather beaten face, causing the monster to stir from its slumber. This particular den had been carefully chosen to provide the greatest protection from the chilly night winds, at the same time allowing good visibility across a wide area of moor. Without moving, the Bog Bouncer could see across to the Pennine Way path, a safe distance away, and deserted at this early hour. Other dens would be used on Bleaklow, depending on weather conditions or human activity, but the numerous clusters of gritstone dotted around the hill, always provided sufficient seclusion for most circumstances.

The Bog Bouncer jumped in shock, as the harsh, deep alarm call of a red grouse shattered the relative peace of the morning. Pecking around the base of the rocks, the grouse had not expected to meet such an unusual creature around the corner. In disbelief, the red grouse strutted away, still croaking, and glaring over its shoulder. Now that the Bog Bouncer was well and truly awake, there seemed little point in sitting around. After a habitual scan in all directions, and a good stretch of its long limbs, the monster bounced effortlessly onto the top of the highest stone, paused for a moment, then leapt an incredible distance onto the springy tussock grass. As if obsessed by some great urgency, the Bog Bouncer shot across the Bleaklow plateau, thoroughly enjoying its early morning romp. With little regard for the treacherous swamps, the Bog Bouncer darted first one way, then the other, always landing safely, and never pausing to adjust its position or gauge the distance before taking off again, over the horizon.

A loan runner approached Bleaklow Head from the northwest. His progress was made more difficult by the strong winds which hit him, head on, causing his anorak to fill like a sail, and threatening to blow him back down the hill. Some distance away the Bog Bouncer keenly watched in great amusement as the runner tackled some of Bleaklow's notorious quagmires. At first he would try to jump across the vast oozing mass, but after several unsuccessful attempts, which almost resulted in disaster, the runner changed his tactics to a more indirect method. The Bog Bouncer was itching to demonstrate his own technique, but decided to remain behind his rock, and enjoy more of the show. At this stage, the word runner would hardly be appropriate, for the combination of wind and water had reduced this stout hearted athlete, to a bedraggled wreck, who now staggered in great circles to avoid the worst of Bleaklow's surprises.

Around the summit area lie many deceptive obstacles to human travellers. Beautiful beds of moorland grass, sometimes red and sometimes brilliant cream, hide a deeper sticky menace around their submerged roots. Steep groughs of black or brown peat seem just possible to cross, while keeping on a vital compass bearing, but the other side is always too steep, too high and too sloppy. Some unfortunate people have been known to wander around for hours in this natural maze, often ending up back in the same place. Perhaps the most frustrating, are the little waterways, separating the few islands of grass and heather. These are unpredictable. A walker could easily mistake a firm footing for a deep peat bog, and end up sinking up to his or her neck.

The Bog Bouncer emerged from its hiding place, now that the runner had disappeared out of sight. The cloud level had lifted slightly, and the low midday sun caused shadows to drift across the hillside. The monster soon found another creature to study. A mountain hare, still in its white winter coat, nibbled cautiously at a clump of heather. It soon became aware that the Bog Bouncer was watching from behind a peat grough, only a few metres away. The hare sat up with its ears erect, and with a few bounds from its powerful hind legs, the hare was soon away from any danger. Of course there was no threat from the Bog Bouncer. This shy, but inquisitive monster had only stopped to admire the mountain hare. The Bog Bouncer had noticed the striking similarities between the hare and itself. Both had powerful long legs which enabled them to travel quickly over the Bleaklow Wilderness. Both had large feet, which prevented them from sinking into the swamp. The Bog Bouncer also had the ability to change its colour like the mountain hare, so that it would be camouflaged against the snow covered hills, during a normal winter.

After the hare had gone, the moor again was deserted. In the distance, the cars and lorries passed by endlessly, along the Snake Road. The Bog Bouncer accepted this noisy invasion through its territory, and occasionally crossed the road at night after the traffic had gone. Similar bouncing areas are found on Kinder Scout, only a few kilometres to the south. These peaty moorlands compare favourably with Bleaklow, but there is always a greater chance of making an embarrassing encounter with the human travellers.

It was not long before the next visitors arrived. Three heavily laden walkers marched impressively along the new Pennine Way Footpath. They stopped for a few moments at a path junction, to check their maps, then started off along the gentle incline towards Bleaklow Head. The group made good progress along the new floating path which had been laid down to prevent excessive erosion along this busy route. The Bog Bouncer had watched every section of this path being installed, and had tested it each night after the workers had gone home. The monster was quite puzzled at first by this new springy path across a favourite piece of marsh, but soon found, that with some experiment and practice, it could achieve an amazing speed, without having to change direction.

The Pennine Way walkers entered the old drain path, known as Devils Dike. The wind, which was stronger than ever, pushed them along towards Hern Stones, (one of the Bog Bouncers regular vantage points). From here the monster could keep a wary eye on several approaches to the moor, and at night when the lights came on in Glossop to the west, the monster would look down, and try to think about that other world in the valley.

As the last strip of daylight disappeared over the western sky, the Bog Bouncer embarked on its final romp, before finding a suitable den for the long January night. At Bleaklow Stones, the monster played an energetic game with an imaginary friend. At first it would bounce around the gritstone tors at high speed, as though in headlong pursuit. This part of the game involved chasing round and round the rocks, between them, over them, and back in the opposite direction. Without warning the Bog Bouncer would suddenly stop at the base of a rock, as though its partner had reached a sanctuary or base (as in tag). The monster would wait patiently, then resume the chase with renewed vigour. Then, as suddenly as the game had begun, the monster would change over with its imaginary friend, and frantically search for safe bases on top of the rocks. This routine could go on for over an hour, and on clear still evenings when dramatic sunsets fill the sky, a lucky observer might glimpse a strange silhouette high up on the dark Bleaklow plateau.

By late evening, the winds had died down to a moderate breeze, but the night clouds blanketed the sky, making it almost as dark as the moor. This would be a good night to face west, towards the warm red glow above Glossop, so the Bog Bouncer settled down with its back against a large gritstone, enchanted by the flickering lights in the distance. As the tiny headlights made their way home along Snake Road, the monster closed its weary eyes, after another eventful day.

"The monster was even grumpier than usual."

It had been a very busy Sunday on Stanage. Hundreds of visitors had swarmed along the edge, enjoying s crisp and clear February day, with magnificent views and a thin covering of snow which made the hills appear to be a dream.

Positioned close to the cliff edge, the Stanage Stomper stood impatiently on its one enormously thick leg, waiting for the last of the visitors to leave. Stars were already shining in the early evening sky, high above Stanage, and an eerie mist slowly rolled down the valley sides. The monster was even grumpier than usual. It had been unable to move all day, due to the endless procession of walkers, runners and sightseers.

One family, without realising, had settled down to eat their lunch next to the monster. Its rough and lumpy skin looked like any other rock near the path. Even the tiny lichens and mosses had been fooled by the appearance of this hulk, as they had colonised the rounded parts of its head and back, making it look like part of the gritstone scenery.

For nearly an hour, the Stanage Stomper tolerated all the bad habits the family could display. One of the children used the monster for target practice. This particularly nasty child had spotted the large rounded shape (which was the monsters belly), and decided that the belly button would make an excellent bulls eye for his fistful of pebbles. This little episode was more annoying than painful for the monster. The mother, who should have been setting a better example for her motley children, thought that their empty tin cans, paper bags and orange peel would fit nicely into the crack between the monsters toes. The father was obviously out to enjoy every moment of his Sunday trip. He made himself comfortable against the Stompers leg, and proceeded to light a pipefull of the most disgusting tobacco imaginable. The thick, acrid clouds of smoke drifted up and filled the monsters eyes. At this point, it had almost decided to stamp out the pipe and its owner, but just as the Stomper was about to move, the man jumped up. His other child had scrambled up onto the monsters head, and was leaning out at a precarious angle over the cliff edge, With a mischievous glint in the monsters eye, it recognised an opportunity not to be missed, and made a shake, just enough to frighten the pimply faced child. The father immediately pounced up to the rescue, still with his pipe spewing out fire. The family gathered up their belongings and left.

The moon was particularly bright, and from where the Stanage Stomper stood, on the high northern part of the edge, a rare and beautiful scene was illuminated to the west. The snow covered hills of Kinder Scout looked wild and spectacular in the distance, but down in the Derwent Valley, a transformation had taken place. The mist had now blanketed the valley floor. Even the enchanting waters of Ladybower had almost disappeared under the ghostly white cover. Only a small sparkling surface remained near the road bridge, and here, the car lights shone, like tiny stars. To the south west, there was no sign of life in the villages below. The lights from cottages and farms normally shine out in the dark, but on this night the mist had extinguished all but the highest of lights. A few solitary hill farms still stood out, like beacons. The constant noise of traffic still drifted up from the valley.

From its lofty vantage point, the Stanage Stomper surveyed the territory. The gritstone edge stretches out for three miles or so, to the south east. This is the monsters main stomping ground. The broad stony path is firm underfoot, and the gradient changes little along its entire length. Only the road crossings to the north and south, prevent the monster from travelling further. Being a very heavy and ungainly creature, the Stanage Stomper normally avoids the steep slopes, if possible. Sometimes, a detour along difficult ground may be necessary, to avoid confrontation with the tourists. Occasionally, when the monster is really grumpy, it will be tempted to stomp down a narrow path to work out in a special corner of Stanage, at the foot of the crags.

On this night the Stanage Stomper felt more irritable than it had been since the summer. Encouraged by the thick cover of mist in the valley below, the monster started out on its long trek, down the well worn path, knowing that the return journey would be slow and hard. Once the initial steps had been taken, the monster started to get into a rhythm, with its heavy foot stomp, stomp, stomping down the path. The frozen snow crunched under the great weight, but soon the slope started to level out, and here the monster left the path, crashing off through the rocks and bracken.

The Stanage Stomper arrived at its special place, under the crags (which loomed black and dominating against the night sky). The moon shone down on a cluster of abandoned millstones laying at various angles on the hillside. These massive sculptures which had been shaped into perfect discs by craftsmen, long ago, were now the adopted playthings of the monster. Feeling exhilarated by its journey down from the edge after a long and frustrating day, the Stanage Stomper first began its training session, by lifting one of the millstones onto its edge. This initial task would have taken the strength of more than ten strong men to manage the deadweight, but the monster coped effortlessly, and proceeded to roll the stone round and round the site, leaving a crazy trail in the snow and bracken. This exercise was only a warm up routine, and was soon followed by a remarkable feat. With lumpy arms stretched out across another millstone, the monster grasped tightly, and raised the giant rock above its head. This required some effort, even for the Stanage Stomper, but one lift was not sufficient to satisfy this powerful creature. One after another of these enormous stones was lifted in exactly the same manner, then replaced carefully in their original positions amongst the frost covered bracken.

By midnight, the Stanage Stomper had returned to the high ground, and looked down over the desolate hillside below the edge. A cool breeze had picked up while the monster had been busily occupied earlier, and dark grey clouds pushed across the sky from the north west. The moon gradually disappeared behind a thickening blanket of cloud, and large snow flakes began to fall over Stanage.

A barn owl silently flew along the line of the crags, looking for small rodents in the scattered rocks below. Its white under-feathers camouflaged the ghostly hunter as it methodically searched the snow covered ground. The Stanage Stomper enjoyed the company of these night visitors, and knew that other regulars would appear before the first light of dawn. An old fox that lived in the rocks at the foot of the edge, had already left the hill earlier in the evening, on its long journey around the lower farms and villages. The monster expected to see her returning back up the hill, in her usual confident manner.

The snow had piled up high on the monsters rounded back, and the breeze had caused the snow to drift against its leg. The Stanage stomper looked more like a snowman, but these wintry conditions did not worry it, and they did not worry the next visitors to the edge. A pair of badgers romped around in the new snow, close to the monster. They acknowledged the presence of the Stanage Stomper in their usual casual way, and continued with their play, chasing and rolling in the snow. The badgers had given up the idea of hunting for the night, in preference to their new, more enjoyable pastime. They had played around the edge for longer than they had originally intended, and as the dawn began to break the badgers realised some sense of urgency. Trotting off towards their set, over on Hallam Moor, they left behind, a scattered trail of chaos, as evidence of their nights activity.

The early morning light revealed a thick covering of snow over Stanage. Even the steep gritstone crags had been plastered white. The Stanage Stomper could see that its deep footprints down the track had been covered over by the heavy snow fall during the night, and the imprints around the millstones had also disappeared.

As lights started to shine from the homes in Hathersage, the local people prepared for a busy Monday morning, clearing the snow from their drives. The familiar sound of car engines drifted up to the edge where the monster stood, as people cautiously began to make their way along the slippery roads to work. Many had to travel into

Sheffield, and all routes in had been blocked by the drifting snow overnight. Even the busy A57 route to the north was still impassable where it crosses the high moor, although snow plough's had been out early, and would soon clear a way through. The Stanage Stomper surveyed the chaos on the roads in utter contentment. The peaceful solitude made such a contrast after Sundays problems. With all access routes to Stanage blocked, the monster could relax and enjoy the whole wilderness, without any disturbances or worries.

The busy summer weekends seemed so far away, but the vivid memory of a particularly stressful incident still flashed back into the monsters mind. Two rock climbers had been eying up a route beneath the Stanage Stomper. They seemed to spend a long time studying their guide book. Perhaps they could not work out the presence of an unfamiliar boulder at the top of the route! Anyway they eventually decided that a top rope would be required, so the Stanage Stomper stopped breathing while a frail looking youth fastened his rope around the monsters leg. The other (heavier) climber tied himself on below, and was soon half way up the rock face. Without warning, the climber lost his grip, and slipped hopelessly off the crag. His partner must have lost his concentration, for he too was pulled off his feet by the shock of the fall. Luckily their belay held them both, but the monsters leg, as tough as it may be, still bears the scar of that rope.

The peaceful interlude in the snow was soon to be interrupted. The farmer and his dog approached along the edge. Most of his sheep were sheltering close to the farm buildings below, but some had wandered back onto the hill. The farmer used his long stick to poke into the drifts for his lost sheep, while his dog helped to sniff around in the snow. The Stanage Stomper recognised this particular sheepdog, by its unusual white patches around both eyes, and knew that trouble was imminent. This dog knew every stone along Stanage Edge, and had long since worked out, that one particular stone tended to move positions from day to day. The farmer was so busy recovering one of his ewes from a hole between the rocks, that he did not notice his dogs unusual behaviour. First it barked then it growled at the monster, in a suspicious sort of way. The Stanage Stomper was more worried by the thought of the farmer, and decided to keep still, while the dog continued to show its disapproval.

Soon the farmer wandered off, back along the edge, holding his struggling sheep under his arm. The monster, being a bit of an opportunist, made a little stomp, and bumped into the sheepdog which had become somewhat tiresome, With its tail between its legs, the dog raced back to its master, in a much quieter and subdued mood. The Stanage Stomper smiled to itself and settled down to enjoy the rest of the day.

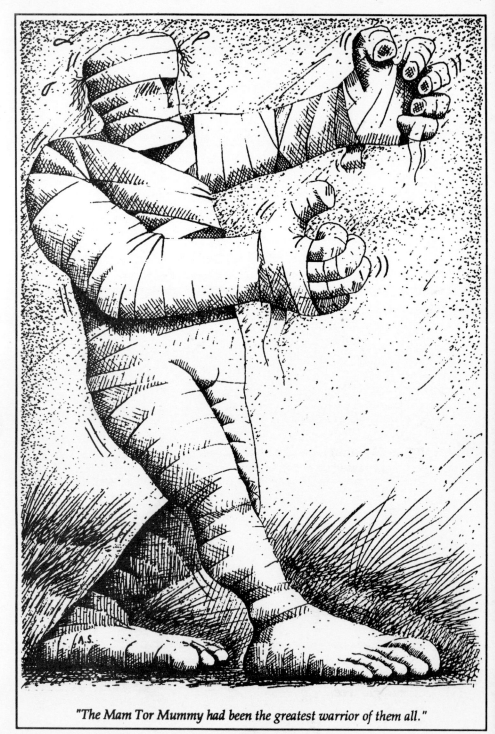

"The Mam Tor Mummy had been the greatest warrior of them all."

CHAPTER
3

THE
MAM
TOR
MUMMY

Deep inside the secret burial chamber beneath Mam Tor, the Mummy stirred from its deep, deep sleep. It had been dreaming about happier days, long ago, but on this miserable March morning, the vibration of studded running shoes on the hill top, sent a shudder through the rocks.

A fell race was in progress, though there was little to see, for the thick hill cloud and wintry drizzle obscured the ridge along which the runners stampeded. They had travelled from far and wide to take part in this gruelling annual event, and some three hundred brave athletes had crossed over the starting line.

Huddled around the summit cairn, a small group of volunteers manned the check point as the runners passed through. Their task was made even more difficult by the poor visibility and driving winds. Competitors numbers had to be checked, and their times recorded. The check point team were so involved in their work, and so busy trying to keep warm, that nobody spared even a moment to consider what strange events happened on the very same spot, a long time ago. Conditions were so atrocious that anyone or 'anything' could pass them by within a few metres without being noticed.

The front runners had chased through, hard on the heels of the leader, but now, an ominous rumble (like thunder) could be heard, as the main mass approached the Mam Tor check point. The Mummy pulled itself up into a sitting position on the cold stone slab where it had been resting. With bandaged hands clutching at its head, the Mummy tried to shut out the noise and vibration, but rock and dust rained down onto the tormented creature from the roof of the chamber. The Mummy decided that enough was enough. Feeling its way along the dark passageways, the Mummy tripped and stumbled, as it rushed to find the opening onto the hill.

Legend says that thousands of years ago, long before the Iron Age settlers on Mam Tor, a powerful and well organised civilisation existed on the hill. They are believed to have commanded the whole region from this lofty stronghold, and sailed their warboats along the deep flooded valleys of Edale and Hope to the Derwent Sea. Ancient maps show the sites of twin ports below Mam Tor, to the north and south of the ridges. From these ports, paved roads allowed their army to gain access onto the ridge at Hollins Cross. Beacons would have been used at strategic points along the ridge, to warn of any invasion.

Due to the limitation of space on Mam Tor, these industrious people apparently made deep excavations into the soft shaly rocks, and carved out a labyrinth of passageways and storage rooms. Burial chambers were created for their great leaders and warriors who died in battle.

The Mam Tor Mummy had been the greatest warrior of them all. Carvings on the walls of its burial chamber tell the story of the giant warrior courageously leading his comrades into battle. Standing more than twice as high as any other soldier on the battlefield, this mighty warrior sliced his way to victory after victory, wielding a long sword of enormous dimension. The carvings show vividly how the giant was eventually felled during combat. A heavy stone missile had struck him on the head, with devastating effect. An immediate retreat was signalled, and their great leader carried back to the hill fort on Mam Tor.

Such was the feeling of sorrow at the loss of their champion, that meticulous preparations were made for the preservation of his body, and all the people were in mourning for many weeks. Politicians, soldiers and common people from all over the land, hearing of the tragedy, travelled many miles to pay their last respects, before the warrior was finally entombed in his lavishly crafted burial chamber.

So the mummified figure laid at rest, surrounded by his possessions and treasures, with his trusty long sword placed firmly in his massive hands. The perfectly preserved giant remained undisturbed for thousands of years, during which time many significant changes had taken place in the region. The great inland seas had long since drained away, leaving deep fertile valleys which were then inhabited by peaceful herdspeople.

Stories passed down from generation to generation, among the country folk of Hope valley, tell of a dramatic eye witness account which occurred centuries ago. An old shepherd who had been out on the slopes of Mam Tor one stormy night had experienced a great shaking and moving of the hillside, as though some powerful being had been fighting to escape from within the mountain. Lightening had illuminated the eastern slopes of Mam Tor, so that the shepherd could see the whole hillside slip away before his eyes. In disbelief, the shepherd watched a giant white monster figure emerge from the rubble, high up on the steep rocky wall. When the figure had stood erect on its two feet, the shepherd decided it was time to retreat into the valley, and tell his tale around the homes and villages.

The massive landslip on the eastern slopes of Mam Tor is clear enough to see today, and geologists would put this down to the natural slipping of sandstone over shales, but only the old shepherd knew what really happened on that stormy night. He had indeed witnessed the Mam Tor Mummy at the new entrance to its passageway, as a result of the land slip. Woken from its suspended animation by the violent thunder storm the Mummy had realised with terror, the situation it was in. Using all its mighty strength, the Mummy had pounded at the stone walls of its burial chamber, until at last, the whole hillside had slipped away on its unstable foundations. A new opening now led directly out onto the inaccessible slope of Mam Tor. Only the great strength and determination of this obsessed creature, would allow it to scale the final wall to the summit.

The Mam Tor Mummy had found its way out into the open, but its confused mind still lived in the past. Unable to find its long lost comrades on the hill top, the Mummy returned to the crumbling remains of its burial chambers, to continue its long sleep.

Only when the storms are particularly violent, or when human activity is especially disturbing, does the Mummy reappear to pace restlessly around the hill. The clatter of ponies hooves or the hacking noises made by the footpath builders, have occasionally resulted in the presence of an unexplained giant. Sometimes when the winter has been really severe, and Mam Tor's face is covered in ice, the climbers come up to test their skills on this formidable wall. These are the times that prove unbearable for the Mam Tor Mummy, for the hammering of pitons into the solid ice, sends piercing vibrations directly into the monster's passageway. Sooner or later, some unsuspecting climber will come face to face with the Mummy, and records will be broken for the fastest descent. Of course no one would ever believe a story like that, but a new route may eventually appear in the guidebook, entitled the Mummy's Face ?

On this cold wet day, the rhythmic thudding of runners' shoes must have sounded like the hill army of long ago, marching to war along the ridge. The similarity was realistic enough, for the Mummy, driven by some powerful force, pulled itself onto the hill top and rushed at reckless speed with arms outstretched into the mist. Frantically seeking to find its battalion, the Mummy moved with enormous strides down the hill towards Hollins Cross, silently passing the weary fell runners by a few metres, as they climbed towards the summit. Each runner was locked in deep concentration, with eyes fixed only at the heels of the next person ahead.

Unnoticed, and bewildered by the unexplained absence of its comrades, the Mummy returned once more to its burial chamber. The hill was peaceful now. The runners and check point officials had long since gone down to the valley. The only movement on Mam Tor was the swirling mist around the summit cairn, and the damp grasses bending in the wind.

"The creature hurtled down into the quagmire."

CHAPTER
4
THE
SNAKE PASS
SLIME
SLITHERER

The Slitherer had found an ideal site for its morning activities, high up amongst the Bleaklow peat groughs. This particular grough had all the qualities necessary for good slithering, with steep, wet sides, and sufficient depth from the heathery start to the sloppy finish.

Crouched on the highest point of the grough, with toes curled around the overhanging heather roots, the Slitherer pushed hard, with all the energy of an Olympic downhill champion. The creature hurtled down into the quagmire with hands and feet flailing at the peat to gain momentum. In ecstasy, it reached the waterlogged bottom with such velocity, that it disappeared into the black oozing mass, and continued fully submerged along the flooded channel.

The Slitherer's body has evolved over thousands of years into a smooth streamlined shape, specifically designed for this energetic tobogganing life style around the Snake Pass slopes. Even its bullet shaped head, and closing nostrils, allow fast movement through these treacherous groughs which present insurmountable problems for most other creatures. Of course, its neighbour the Bleaklow Bog Bouncer has adopted a different but equally successful method of travelling across this heavily dissected plateau.

Conditions were perfect on this wet April morning. The peat groughs were already flooded, after several weeks of storms and showers. A series of depressions had crossed the Atlantic in rapid succession, piling heavy rain clouds against the Pennine slopes. Rain lashed across the moor as the Slitherer pulled itself out of the mire, covered from head to foot in disgusting black slime. This creature looks decidedly repulsive at the best of times, but with its covering of sticky Bleaklow peat, the Slitherer would find few admirers. Feeling exhilarated after such a lengthy toboggan run, it could hardly wait to clamber up to the top again for another attempt. Although the steep sided groughs may be ideal for sliding down, they are certainly not designed for climbing up, even for a Slime Slitherer. The heavy rain had lubricated the slopes to such an extent that the creature found it could only manage to scramble half way up, before slithering back down again. After several unsuccessful attempts, the Slitherer gave up this line of ascent, and splashed its way along the grough to find an easier way up.

A few minutes later, a shiny clean monster reappeared at the top of its toboggan run. The torrential rain had washed away every trace of peat, revealing its mottled green skin. The Slitherer paused for a moment to survey the landscape. It considered the abundant options for slithering. The southern Bleaklow slopes, being the monsters favourite territory, offer countless groughs and waterways. These have all been tried and tested in varying conditions of wetness. The monster's eye caught sight of an attractive looking slope some distance away across the Snake road. This bleak expanse of moorland is called Featherbed Moss, and its numerous tiny rivulets twinkled temptingly across the pass from where the Slitherer was crouching.

With a new destination fixed firmly in mind, it set out in a southerly direction, eagerly anticipating the adventures which lay ahead. The Slitherer has developed an amazing ability to navigate accurately across this difficult terrain. As though guided by some inbuilt sense of direction, the creature slipped down into the deep grough, clambered up and over the next obstacle, then down a little waterway, always heading relentlessly for its chosen place. This is no easy task, as many humans have discovered to their dismay. Even armed with detailed map and compass, the Bleaklow peat groughs have an annoying habit of disorientating people. These deep twisting gulleys all look very similar, and once down in the bottom of the grough, there is no reliable means of telling which way to go. The view from the top of the grough is often no great help, as the monotonous, featureless skyline seems to spread out endlessly. On a clear day, the problems are enough to deter most sound minded travellers, but in foggy conditions and at night, this exposed wilderness is best left to the Slime Slitherer and other creatures that call it their home.

As the Slitherer came closer to the busy Snake Pass road, it slipped down a steep stream channel, taking advantage of the little pools along the way, then gliding between the stones in the deeper stretches near to the grassy bank. At a bend in the stream, the Slitherer noticed some sheep, grazing close to the water amongst the reeds. This seemed like an opportunity for a little fun. Having a naturally playful temperament the Slime Slitherer is easily tempted into any game that can be invented along the way. Approaching the nearest sheep, whilst underwater the Slitherer stealthily pulled up close to the overhanging bank, and sent a spray of water with its broad webbed hand, over the startled sheep. Looking through a clump of reeds to observe the sheep's reaction, the Slitherer chuckled to itself, then slipped silently beneath the water again, with a premeditated plan. This time it glided up close to another unsuspecting ewe, which was enjoying the grass on the bankside, with its head only inches away from the water. The Slitherer popped its ugly head out of the water, directly in front of the sheep. This was enough to make the sheep jump clear of the ground. The ewes, sensing this sudden alarm signal, bolted for the safety of a steep grassy slope, where they gazed around restlessly before resuming their lunch.

With some anxiety, the Slitherer viewed the traffic passing by, from the safety of a roadside embankment. It had suspected problems with the road crossing, and had taken this into account with the choice of route. Any attempt at a daytime crossing would be extremely risky for this lizard like amphibious creature. Although its movements may be amazingly fast in the water, its efficiency is severely restricted when tarmac surfaces are encountered. The Slitherer had almost come to grief on several occasions, in its impulsive desire to try out fresh slithering grounds across the Snake Pass road. Consequently, this elusive creature has grown in wisdom, and now crosses only at night, when the road is not so busy, or at chosen points, where the storm drains allow easy passage through to the other side.

The Slitherer slipped down from the embankment to inspect a particular drain which had been conveniently placed for its migratory route. With daylight clearly visible at the far end of the concrete drain, the Slitherer swam through in the dark flood water. Framed by the round exit, the rivulets cascaded down the waterlogged hillside ahead. Within minutes, this highly mobile monster was well clear of the noise and clutter on the road, and revelled in the watery delights of Featherbed Moss.

A merlin approached from the south west. It had been flying low over the moor in search of its favourite prey, the meadow pipit, and now followed every curve of a little tributary stream, like a fighter pilot. With calculated speed, the bird rounded a rocky spur, only to be confronted with the Slime Slitherer at very close quarters. Turning instantly, in mid flight, the little falcon shot away, leaving the monster to admire its aerobatic agility.

Looking back across the Snake road to Bleaklow, the Slitherer felt a twinge of restlessness. It realised that these days of fun and games would soon be over. Each year, towards the end of May, the Slitherer hibernates through the drier summer months, when the stream beds are reduced to a trickle. The monster would soon find a suitably sloppy peat grough, where a tunnel could be excavated. Pushing head first, with its webbed hands and feet scooping at the peat, the Slitherer can soon disappear out of sight. Only when the tunnel is made deep into the side of the grough, will the entrance be sealed. Curled up inside, on its soft bed of moist peat, the Slitherer will slumber away, insulated from the dry summer winds and the heat of the sun that cracks the dried up surface. Walkers may pass through the grough within a few metres of the hidden tunnel, but no one would suspect, or even consider the possibility of such a strange phenomenon. The inquisitive meadow pipit and the keen eyed merlin would keep the secret until October, when the Slime Slitherer emerges, refreshed after its long hibernation, and ready to explore once again.

" *A large and powerful Glider flapped noisily down towards the most prestigious ledge.*"

CHAPTER
5
THE
GLOSSOP
GLIDER

The high gritstone crags at Kinder Downfall were bathed in a dull red glow as the sun sank deeper in the western sky. Already, the monsters had come down to roost on the airy ledges near the waterfall. The largest and most dominant monster had established itself on a high ledge, where it enjoyed the warmth of the last rays of sun. It sat in a majestic posture, looking scornfully down on the smaller gliders which had reluctantly occupied the remaining positions in the cool shadows below.

The monsters looked up; they were aware that the sky had suddenly darkened somewhat. A large and powerful glider flapped noisily down towards the most prestigious ledge, its massive outstretched wings almost blocking out the remaining light. The dominant monster felt more and more agitated as this determined young giant approached, intent on winning the prized position. Again and again, its bony legs lunged and kicked, but each attempt was thwarted by the dominant monster's superior skills. Eventually, the overgrown juvenile gave up its courageous efforts, and settled down on the next available ledge, some distance below.

The lofty gritstone crags of Kinder Downfall, provide an ideal roost for the Glossop Gliders. Dark, precipitous walls adjacent to the waterfall, offer an abundance of secure ledges, and the breathtaking drop below the crags, enables the monsters to take off directly, without any danger of damaging their enormous wings on rocks or other obstacles.

A steady flow of ochre coloured water poured over the big gritstone slabs at the top of the falls. This was not as spectacular as it had been during the spring, when the meltwater from the high plateau, discharged into the River Kinder and over the falls with thundering force. A light spray now blew up into the air above the falls as updraughts caught the water, sending constant showers down over the roosting monsters, and making shiny patterns on their dark leathery skins. The evening was mild and calm, and a bright moon shone down onto the western edge of Kinder

Scout. Only a gentle gurgling of the river broke the silence of the night above the falls, but down in the dark ravine of Kinder Downfall, a deafening screeching and squawking continued, as these restless, irritable monsters squabbled, above the constant noise of the waterfall.

Below Kinder Downfall, tiny lights flickered over the vast populated plain, with the brightest glow to the north west, where Manchester and its surrounding towns and villages, displayed their presence in the night sky. Nearer to the hills lie the settlements of Hayfield, New Mills and Glossop, the latter giving its name to the monsters which annually visit this area. In the summer months, the Glossop Gliders soar high in the sky, especially around the western edges of Kinder, taking advantage of rising thermals. Their enormous wings, which may be more than six metres across, allow effortless flight, like the eagle that once inhabited this territory.

Being near the end of May, this small flock of Gliders had only recently arrived in the Peaks, having migrated northwards in search of suitable warm conditions. Sightings of the monster have been recorded as far north as the Cuillin Mountains of Skye, although this particular summer had been exceptionally hot, and temperatures must have attracted them well beyond their normal range. An ornithologist in the Trent Valley had also written a full description of the Gliders, as he observed them high in the sky through his binoculars. This sighting is likely to have been made as the monsters homed in towards the Derbyshire hills. The ornithologist must have been very excited by his discovery, for large eagle-like birds are rarely seen in this lowland area. One of the largest birds to frequent the Trent Valley, is the grey heron, and even this seems diminutive, compared with the Glossop Gliders. Apart from these occasional sightings, little else is known of their migratory routes, or their wintering area.

Just a few wing beats away from the roost, lies Rushup Edge. The monsters had spent a few interesting hours here during the previous day, where they encountered some hang gliders above the northern slopes. As the morning had been warm and sunny, the Glossop Gliders had aimlessly drifted across Kinder, making great circles, high up in the clear blue sky. As they passed over the grassy slopes of Rushup Edge, they noticed some tiny colourful shapes, which seemed to be moving, a long way below. Puzzled by these bright airborne objects which stood out against the greens and browns of the hills, the monsters slowly descended to investigate. Rather like vultures, patiently circling over a dying animal, the Glossop Gliders dropped closer and closer, but they had no intention of interfering with the humans. A pair of crows came too close for comfort for a few moments, as they tried to scare these large unwelcome visitors away from their territory. Of course the hang gliders were too busy concentrating on keeping in the air, to notice this little skirmish, not too far above their heads. A small group of spectators on Mam Tor, looked up in amazement, and then looked at each other in disbelief.

Sometimes a juvenile Glossop Glider would follow the train as it noisily made its way along the Edale Valley, but at Barber Booth, some confusion would occur as the train disappeared into the tunnel. This strange act of magic, could often cause the monster to panic, and make irregular swoops and dives to try and find out what happened to the train. It may take several days to discover the secret of the disappearing trains, but eventually the young Glider would notice the familiar sight of the passenger coaches reappearing on the western side of Colborne ridge. The monsters may then spend hours around this location, chasing trains along the Edale Valley, and then racing over the hill to beat the engine to the tunnel entrance. This little game is usually played at high altitude, far out of sight of the passengers who gaze sleepily at the fields passing rapidly by.

In the twilight of the early hours, the monsters fidget and adjust their leathery wings, never remaining still. In a short time they would be taking off for their early morning flight. With just a rustle of their great wings, these spectacular monsters will leave their roost in the half light of the early morning, and aim out over Kinder Reservoir to Hayfield and New Mills where all is quiet and still. From here they may take a northerly circuit of Glossop and Longdendale, or depending on their mood, a southerly route via Whaley Bridge and Buxton.

With the long, warm summer ahead of them, the Glossop Gliders take each day as it comes, without the cares and worries of the world they see down in the valley. The monsters take advantage of their freedom to roam the Peaks at will.

"It's swivelling eyes, like a submarine's periscope, observed the fisherman."

The old fisherman had positioned himself off a rocky headland on the southern branch of Ladybower Reservoir. He had waded out quite a way so that he could cast in several directions where the fish were rising. Behind him, the dark forested slopes rose steeply to the craggy summit of Win Hill. It was a calm June day. The water rippled smoothly, and lapped around the rocks near the edge. Rainbow trout were greedily feeding on flies at the surface, and the fisherman looked around excitedly, his keen eyes alert for a big rise within his casting range. A steady rhythmical swish of the fisherman's rod, sent his line out effortlessly, with each cast sending the fly accurately into the reservoir.

The Lurker stealthily paddled close up to the old fisherman, being careful not to cause any movement at the surface of the water. The monster could see the man tying on a new fly, and chose this opportunity to push its little trunk out of the water, to take a breath of air. At the same time, its swivelling eyes, like a submarine's periscope, observed the fisherman's position at a glance, then silently vanished from sight. The old fisherman had spotted the Lurker, several minutes ago, but played along, as though he had not noticed. Over the seasons at Ladybower, he had become wise to the monster's inquisitive and playful behaviour, and a secret rapport existed between them.

The Lurker did not restrict its games to the shoreline. Much fun was to be had around the fishermens' rowing boats, out in the open water. With a controlled flick of its hand, the monster could expertly create a ring on the water's surface, just like the rise of some giant brown trout which had escaped the hooks and grown to an immense size. The fishermen would immediately divert their attention to this wonderful opportunity, and cast to the very centre of the rise. By this time, the monster would have slipped cunningly under the boat, and popped up at the other side to enjoy the entertainment, as the fishermen frantically tried in vain to hook the prize-winner. Sometimes, the Lurker may playfully send a jet of water over the fishermens' backs, or mischievously turn the boat around.

This large freshwater mammal is well adapted to lurking secretively, in this popular visitors' area. Its stubby little trunk allows the monster to breath without being detected. Its large webbed hands are capable of rotating the Lurker through all manner of positions, rather like the underwater movements of a synchronised swimmer, although its actions are distinctly evasive, rather than aesthetic.

How the creature arrived here is still a mystery, for the valleys were only flooded in the nineteen forties, and prior to this dramatic event, the lowlands were farmed and populated. This relatively short space of time to the present day, is hardly long enough to account for the evolution of such a marvellous species, which seems so at home in its man made lake. Some convincing explanations will be left to the scientists, but it is worth noting that the Ladybower Lurker is amphibious, as mentioned later on.

The northern limb of Ladybower Reservoir offers unrestricted potential for 'speeding', and here the monster excels. Its favourite pastime, when there are no fishermen to pester, is to swim at high speed along the lake, with hands paddling away at its side, and its powerful tail making dolphin-like thrusts. The wake created by this activity often causes eyebrows to be raised, and questions to be asked. It is not unusual to see scores of people scattered along the banks of the reservoir, with their high powered binoculars and cameras, hoping to catch sight of the breathtaking event.

Life is not always so free and easy for this amiable monster. The summer months often have their dry periods, when stream beds become exposed to wind and sun, and the water level in the reservoir drops day after day. The problem became so severe in the summer of 1959 that even the remains of old villages on the floor of the reservoir, became exposed once again. These are times of great anxiety for the Lurker, and some years have seen the water so low, that there has barely been sufficient depth for the monster to survive.

Fortunately, these extremely dry conditions rarely last long enough to cause serious problems, and at other times, the rains or melting snow can have the opposite effect. It is during these periods of flood water, that the Ladybower lurker is really in its element. Streams in full spate pour down from the hills, and discharge into the reservoir, causing powerful currents and eddies. Great sporting opportunities are plentiful for the monster when the reservoir is brimmed full. Near Ladybower dam are two massive overflow ducts which allow floodwater to escape before it can flow over the dam wall. These great circular openings drain the excess water, rather like a bath plug hole, and anything that happens to be floating in the water, is drawn towards them and sucked down. Sometimes the Lurker will courageously challenge the overflow to find out which has the stronger pull. The monster will swim closer and closer, until the force of the water becomes so great, that a decision must be made to retreat. Split second timing is essential for the success of this insane activity, which leaves no room for error of judgment. The very fact that the Lurker survives these dare devil stunts, tells us something of its steely personality.

The crooked western finger of the reservoir, points along the narrow valley of the River Ashop, where only a handful of homes cling to the rugged hillside. Not too far upstream from the reservoir, is a hostel overlooking the river. Normally this haven is too far out of reach to be of interest to the monster, but during times of flood, the River Ashop becomes swollen and the reservoir backs up the valley, extending the possibilities for exploration and adventure. Attracted by the lights at the hostel, the Lurker has occasionally been tempted to pull itself out of the flooded river, and struggle up the grassy slope to try and catch a glimpse through the windows. The young people inside having fun and games would be enough to make the monster's eyes swivel, but its trunk pressing against the glass would soon cover the window in its steamy breath. Eventually, the hostel dogs become aware of the night prowler, and their barking signals an appropriate time for the monster to disappear. An observant hosteller may later find some unusual webbed hand prints, or a trail of flattened grass leading back down the slope to the river.

By midday, the old fisherman had given up any possibility of catching a rainbow trout for his dinner. The playful Lurker had been exceptionally mischievous all morning, and had done its best to chase away the fish, and tangle his line. At one point, the monster had misjudged the speed of the fisherman's fly shooting through the water, and found itself in an embarrassing situation, with the hook snagged in the side of its trunk. For a painful minute, its webbed fingers struggled to remove the hook, and several fishermen nearby, looked on in amazement, as the old man's rod bent over at an alarming angle. To his relief, the line became slack and the spectators were left with a story of 'the one that got away'.

As the old fisherman walked back to his car, along the edge of the reservoir, he noticed again that he was not alone. A familiar wake kept pace with him, almost to the footbridge, then, without warning, a big webbed hand appeared out of the water, and flicked a beautiful trout onto the path at the fisherman's feet. Without hesitating, he dropped the fish into his bag, and looked round to say thank you, but the water was still as far as he could see. The old fisherman suddenly became more cheerful, and a spring came into his step as he visualised his dinner sizzling away under the grill.

"The Beauty chuckled to herself as the young man approached."

CHAPTER
7
THE BROWN KNOLL BEAUTY

She sat alone on the hill, amongst the waving grasses and heather. A warm wind from the south blew her beautiful long hair, and big white clouds raced across the sky. The strong sun warmed her shoulders, then momentarily disappeared behind a cloud, causing patches of shadow to move along the hillside. Just across the head of the valley, high up on the edge of Kinder, the rocky outcrops known as 'Wool Packs', stood out against the ever changing sky. Strong rays of sun pushed through gaps in the clouds like spotlights searching along the moor, causing the rocks to change from light to dark.

Even on a warm summer's day, Brown Knoll is not the sort of place that people can get excited about. This windswept summit is dull and featureless, and merely provides a high level link for people wishing to travel from the more spectacular Mam Tor ridge to the vast wilderness of Kinder Scout to the north. The Brown Knoll Beauty appreciated this remote vantage point, and from where she sat, the magnificent panorama of the Edale skyline kept her bemused for hours, while she patiently waited for her next victim.

Being a pleasant July day, the tops were quite busy with walkers and runners passing in both directions over Brown Knoll and Colborne Ridge. A wide grassy path has developed here, where hikers have detoured further and further from the original route, to avoid the marshes and peat bogs. Nearly all the travellers walked with head down and eyes fixed just a few yards ahead, always ready to jump or sidestep the never ending trail of watery obstacles. If some had looked just a short distance away from the path, they may have noticed the striking outline of the Brown Knoll Beauty, sitting in the long grasses, with her tanned shoulders shining in the sun, and her slim, shapely figure displaying such perfect posture.

A young Scotsman of athletic build, approached Brown Knoll from the south. Unlike the other people, he was following a line, well to the east of the main track, and his course brought him unwittingly, closer and closer to the 'Beauty'. The young man was travelling light, with only a small pack, and the spring in his step suggested he was fit and full of vigour. Although he was concentrating mainly on where he was putting his feet, he frequently glanced ahead to check his progress, then with a start, he noticed the unexpected shape of a seated, woman like figure, not too far ahead. For several moments the young man hesitated, then hardly believing his good fortune in finding by chance, what seemed to be such an attractive young lady, he marched on with renewed virility towards the seated 'Beauty'.

Well aware of the people passing to and fro, the 'Beauty' chuckled to herself as the young man approached. This unfortunate hiker would soon be confronted with the creature - half woman, half beast, whose appearance from a distance is so deceptive and inviting. As though she is playing some sort of cruel game, the Brown Knoll Beauty always sits with her back to the unsuspecting victim, her face hidden from view, and shrouded by her beautiful black, flowing hair.

The 'Beauty' may spend much of the long summer season, engaged in this repulsive activity, though many days or weeks may pass before a suitable male is found, wandering off the beaten track. During the daytime, the creature normally sits for hours in a well chosen place, where she can look out along the paths to Edale Cross and Colborne. Occasionally, she may see a hiker far in the distance, moving along a different line, causing her to move position and intercept. Sometimes, thick mists swirl around the hills for days, bringing problems and benefits for the Brown Knoll Beauty. Poor visibility tends to keep people off the hill, resulting in reduced chances of success, but some keen navigators find these conditions advantageous for practising their compass skills. Realising these strange human habits, the 'Beauty' often moves up close to the main path, in the hope of meeting one of these enthusiasts coming through the mist.

Several unexplained incidents have occurred on Brown Knoll; all of them involving solitary male walkers or runners. Some have been found in a state of intense distress or shock, wandering aimlessly around the hill, or sitting as though paralysed near the path. All have been rendered speechless, or unable to speak in a coherent way. Some have lost control of their senses, as sometimes happens when the human mind can not cope with a powerfully stressful situation.

One year, during a fell race, a leading runner came face to face with the Brown Knoll Beauty. He had been seen with the leading group, and was expected to run a fast time, but he did not appear at the finishing line. His friends, suspecting that some sort of accident must have happened, quickly organised a search party to return to the place where he was last seen. They found their comrade crawling around on his hands and knees, amongst the moorland grasses, quietly singing to himself, and incapable of making any normal response. He was stretchered down to the valley, and then off to hospital, but it was several weeks before he came out of his trance. Even after his return to work and normal life, he still had no recollection of his encounter on Brown Knoll. Some of his fell-running friends joked with him about his unusual behaviour on the hill, but although he did not give up running, he chose not to run in that particular race again.

As the young Scotsman came within just a few yards of the 'Beauty', his heart began beating with excitement. At this point, the trap was almost set. Her enticing appearance had attracted the man to take a closer look at this delightful creature, sitting so serenely in the cotton grass. Then, with hauntingly beautiful voice she started to sing with the wind; a soft and enchanting melody, but with sounds of no human origin. The Scotsman knelt down beside her, and as she felt his warm breath on her shoulder, she suddenly turned her face on him, revealing a hideous formless shape. Her wrinkled skin hung grotesquely in folds, and a mass of warts and growths protruded from her bulbous forehead to the end of her shapeless nose. The creatures lower jaw dropped open as she started to laugh. Her revolting, leathery tongue dangled uncontrollably from her mouth as the laughter changed to a cruel cackle. The Scotsman slumped further and further to the ground, helplessly looking up in horror, and beside him, the Brown Knoll Beauty screamed hysterically in hilarious amusement.

"The creature continues to stalk the Dovedale paths to the present day."

CHAPTER
8
THE DOVEDALE DEADHEAD

Long ago, before roads were built to bring tourists into Dovedale, a legendary highwayman instilled fear into all travellers who would dare to chance a journey through the dale. Armed with pistol and staff, the tall hooded figure would lay in wait for wealthy folk, and those who used the packhorse route to transport their goods. This lone vagabond soon gained such a reputation that local people were afraid to travel through the valley, and trade between the towns and villages was badly affected.

Stories passed down from generation to generation tell of a trap set by a rich and famous merchant from Ashbourne. This wealthy gentleman used the Dovedale packhorse route regularly as a means of delivering his produce to markets in the area, and large sums of money and other valuables were often carried in the saddle bags. So much silver and gold had been lost that the merchant decided to put a stop to the highwayman's reign of terror.

Hidden inside a covered cart, the merchant's armed men patiently waited for the signal to attack, then without mercy they cut down the Dovedale Highwayman, leaving him to die by the side of a stony track. News travelled fast around the dales and local people once again ventured out without fear.

Being a miserable and lonely person in his criminal life, the highwayman had no friends or family to mourn him, or to give him a decent burial. His wretched soul was never laid to rest, and his decaying body remained in its half dead state. The creature continues to stalk the Dovedale paths to the present day, as it had done in its previous life.

Occasionally, the 'Deadhead' can be seen stumbling along the well trodden tourist path beside the river, with shoulders slumped forward and arms hanging limp.

Closer inspection would reveal that this is more of a walking skeleton, though fortunately for the visitors, it passes by unnoticed. Unlike the walkers of today who look around with interest at Dovedale's spectacular rock formations or study the trout as they hang in the clear water below the weirs, the creature moves along aimlessly. Its dead eyes see nothing and only a faint memory from the past keeps the 'Deadhead' imprisoned in the steep walled valley. With impassable stepping stones over the river at the south end of the dale, and habitation to the north, beyond Milldale's packhorse bridge, it remains locked in a time capsule, where so many people lost their purses in the past.

During busy August days, the Dovedale Deadhead becomes tormented by the volume of tourists surging along the paths, and seeks seclusion in the many caves along the valley sides. Some of these had been used as hiding places, when as a highwayman he cunningly waited for unsuspecting travellers, or in times of trouble when he needed to lay low after a particularly greedy or bloodthirsty hold up. The Deadhead could slip away from sight along the limestone tunnels, and reemerge further along the valley, using its well tested labyrinth of natural passageways. In the summer months, a dense blanket of vegetation covers the dale-floor and mature woodland thrives on the lower slopes. This abundance of foliage so close to the riverside path, provides additional security for the creature.

On one traumatic occasion, an amateur geologist had been crawling along one of the limestone tunnels, and had come face to face with the Dovedale Deadhead. The young man's headlamp shone directly onto the grisly face, and the intensity of his light revealed maggots swarming inside his mouth, and worms slithering from the eye sockets. Rotting green flesh hung from the creature's partly exposed skull, and long yellow fingernails clutched at the bare rock. The distressed geologist had retreated back along the narrow tunnels, and rushed away to notify the search and rescue team. After many hours of searching, the team found no trace of any partly decomposed body as described by the geologist, and many embarrassing questions were asked after this fruitless call-out.

Visitors frequently arrive at Dovedale in all shapes and sizes, and in all manner of unusual outfits. It is not surprising that the 'Deadhead' can co-exist in this popular place, undetected. It shares the well frequented beauty spots with families, school parties, and ramblers, who may have travelled from far afield to enjoy their excursion into the Peak District's famous valley.

The creature may sit, huddled in a dark corner of 'Dove Holes' caves, with a hood covering its obscene features, while a young family, just an arm's reach away, happily eat their packed lunch under the sheltering overhang of this great limestone hollow. The children may even scramble around, over its feet, or try to squeeze past its bony frame, without realising the horror beneath the ragged garment.

Nearby at Ilam Rock, a shady cave attracts inquisitive visitors, who can not resist the temptation to step inside its mysterious entrance. Here the 'Deadhead' frequently rubs shoulders with numerous people, who stumble around in the half light, trying to tread carefully on the uneven floor. They are more concerned about keeping their feet dry, and have no thoughts about other individuals who may be sharing their gloomy space.

Further down the valley, the path is forced to rise over a rocky limestone spur, where a steep drop to the river must have had some attraction in the past, as it is known locally as 'Lovers' Leap'. The 'Deadhead' often rests at this point after its struggle up the path, and may sit for quite a long time, with skull supported in its rotting hands. It is likely that other unfortunate travellers have willingly made this tragic leap, after coming face to face with this gruesome creature.

Then, on one quiet Sunday evening in late August, as the dusky sky darkened the valley, a wealthy looking couple in their expensive walking gear, set out over the packhorse bridge from Milldale, aiming to walk down the valley before nightfall. The weekend visitors and day trippers had gone, leaving the Dale peaceful, yet strange, in the fading light. A chilly breeze sent a shiver down their spines, and the couple gripped hands tightly, as they sensed a different atmosphere. Soon after they entered the Dale, they became aware of a lone figure, following at a brisk pace. Glancing back, they noticed that he walked with a large wooden staff which rattled on the stony path, sending echoes through the valley. The couple felt uneasy as the clatter of the stranger's staff became louder, and they wished he would pass by to leave them in peace again. As the man turned his head to say 'good evening' to the stranger, his eyes widened in horror, as he found himself looking into the hood of the Dovedale Deadhead. The couple cowered, and raised their hands, as the highwayman once again closed in on his victims with staff and pistol at the ready.

"It's clamping teeth are especially important for negotiating overhanging ledges."

CHAPTER
9
THE
CURBAR
CLAMBERER

The first cars pulled up below Curbar Edge at the start of a promising day. A lethargic bunch of college students emerged from their rusty old vehicle, stretched, and casually gathered together their ropes, hardware and other assorted items. Obviously suffering from a long night at the bar, they made hard work of their climb through the bracken to the foot of the crags. Their movements looked automatic, as they set about their task.

Nearby, the Curbar Clamberer looked on with interest from its lofty position high up on the rock. This small and extremely agile creature had been active since first light, as usual, and had visited most parts of the crag within its territory. A well practised routine each morning keeps the little monster in prime condition as it swarms up and down the crags with ease, spending more time on its favourite routes which are mastered to perfection. Now, the 'Clamberer' clung effortlessly to the gritstone, rather like a spider, keeping still but alert and fully aware of the activity below.

Soon the crags would be overflowing with climbers and ramblers, making the most of a dry September day. The Curbar Clamberer, as yet undetected, thrives on all this company and makes no attempt to hide away. This unusually dexterous creature can move rapidly across the crag face then stay quite still, close to the climbers without being seen. It often gets into mischief and loves to play tricks. One of its favourite games is pebble flicking. After plenty of practice, this cheeky monster has become quite skilful, and loves the resounding noise when a pebble hits a climber's helmet. The prank is even more entertaining as the bewildered person looks around to see where the missiles are coming from.

One of the young climbers in the group was progressing well on a route with plenty of holds and cracks for protection. He seemed unaware that he was being closely studied by the 'Clamberer' who had found a suitable ledge on which to sit near the top of the crag. The monster waited for this unsuspecting climber to come up to the ledge, then as his hand reached up to find a hold, the 'Clamberer' nipped his finger. With a yell of pain, he 'peeled off' backwards, though fortunately his rope held before he could fall. Clinging desperately to the rock, the young climber shouted down to his companion that he had been bitten by a snake, and with no time wasted, the route was descended, leaving slings and wedges hanging from the crag. As the students moved along in search of a less traumatic climb, the little monster looked down, feeling pleased and somewhat exhilarated after achieving some success so early in the day.

Curbar Edge with its spectacular gritstone crags has become home and playground for the 'Clamberer'. It has little need to travel more than a few hundred metres, but occasionally ventures in search of fresh clambering territory along Froggatt Edge to the north, and Baslow Edge to the south. When it needs a break from climbing, the little monster can squeeze into a crack and enjoy the view out over the Derwent Valley, with the villages of Calver and Curbar not very far away.

During quiet periods of the year, or on days when foul weather keeps people away from the hills, the little monster tends to linger around the crags at the southern end of Curbar Edge near the point where a steep road winds its way up to the moor. Here the 'Clamberer' can watch every vehicle with anticipation, and at times when cars stop near the crags, it becomes very excited. Rather like a puppy making a fuss, it will scamper around, up and down the rocks, swinging from one hold to another with apparent recklessness, but always perfectly timed and controlled. Sometimes if the climbers take too long in coming up to the edge, the little monster will lose patience and romp down the boulder strewn slope to take a closer look, being careful to avoid the deep bracken which must seem like a jungle to this diminutive creature. Fortunately the birch trees and boulders at the foot of the crag provide ample aids for rapid movement up and down the slope.

Even though the Curbar Clamberer spends many hours clinging onto the gritstone crags watching the climbers coming and going, it remains unnoticed, yet these enthusiasts would surely be envious if they could see its acrobatic manoeuvres. With amazing strength for its bodyweight, the 'Clamberer' makes light work of even the most extreme situations. Its long arms and legs are supple enough to find holds that would be far too awkward for humans, and its powerful grip has proved more than capable of holding vice-like onto tiny pebbles protruding from the rock face. Manufacturers of rock boots could learn a few lessons from the roughened texture of the monster's feet. Perhaps its most useful attributes are the clamping teeth which are especially important for negotiating overhanging ledges. With teeth firmly attached to the rock, the monster is free to rotate its body up and over exposed ledges, while making use of its gripping souls to walk up the smoothest of faces.

At night, and during the long winter months when conditions are too severe even for this hardy little creature, it curls up to sleep deep inside the dark cracks of Curbar

44

Edge. Often it will take over an abandoned jackdaw's nest for extra comfort, and may share its den with these noisy birds. The jackdaws have become so accustomed to the strange habits of the Curbar Clamberer that they tolerate its impish tricks. Like other diverse creatures of the wild, they co-exist in harmony because of their mutual arrangement to sound the alarm if unwelcome visitors come too close.

It was not long before some more climbers appeared on the scene. They did not carry the bundles of equipment and ropes that other climbers were using, but casually strolled along in vests and shorts, eying up the routes with keen interest. The 'Clamberer' had watched this couple on other occasions, and felt a tingle of excitement as it anticipated some skillful climbing about to take place.

They stopped at the foot of a formidable crag which seemed sheer and totally void of holds, other than the occasional pebble or dimple here and there. If this was not sufficient to terrify even the most capable of climbers, it had yet another obstacle in the form of an overhang of immense proportion, right at the top of the gritstone wall.

With obvious confidence which only comes from years of experience and hard training, this elite pair started moving up the vertical crag, side by side, finding a finger hold here and a friction hold there. At about fifty feet, the girl was slightly higher than her companion, and at this point, something caught her eye. A movement to the left nearly caused her to fall, and as she turned her head, the little monster looked towards the climbers from its position just a few feet away. The girl smiled to her boyfriend, and acknowledged their unexpected company with a nod. This was no place for introductions or conversations, so in unison the three moved up towards the crux, each with total concentration and commitment.

The shadowy overhang loomed closer, and realising their exposed situation, being totally unaided, with certain death a hundred feet below, the couple hesitated before their final effort. Relishing the chance to perform its favourite manoeuvre, the Curbar Clamberer clamped onto the protruding ledge with vice-like teeth, and effortlessly moved up to finish. Exhilarated by such a masterly demonstration, the couple continued with renewed courage to complete their climb.

Pulling themselves over the final ledge, they looked forward to congratulating their new found hero, but soon realised they were alone. Only the distant chatter of climbers could be heard and the metallic clang of their karabiners on the gritstone. Did this young couple really witness a creature with such startling ability and flare ? Other climbers have occasionally encountered strange unknown beasts, though not at such close range as this, and not in this region of the Peak District. Perhaps their secret will be kept for a little longer, or until the 'Clamberer' makes itself known once more to some other fortunate climber.

"The Cavern Crawler can quickly make its way
to all corners of its underground kingdom."

CHAPTER
10
THE
CAVERN
CRAWLER

Deep beneath the ground, in the heart of Derbyshire's limestone country, the monster lay at rest in its master lair. In total blackness and silence, the Cavern Crawler tunes in to its surroundings and remains as always in a high state of readiness for any eventuality. Though it can not see, for it has no eyes, the creature can feel and recognise every inch of its cold stone world.

This particular den has not been chosen by chance. Only after many years of searching has this highly mobile creature found such a strategic site. With tunnels leading off in several directions, the Cavern Crawler can quickly make its way to all corners of its underground kingdom. Even the slightest noise several miles away at a cave entrance or other opening, is immediately registered with the monster which has no trouble in distinguishing between the soft movements of the fox, and the careless stumbles of humans.

Far to the north of its favourite lair are the show caves and caverns of the Castleton area, but even at such a distance away, the Cavern Crawler recognises the familiar sounds and vibrations of steel gates opening and closing, and boots resounding on the stone steps. Visitors to these caverns arrive in their hundreds throughout the year and follow their guides along the illuminated passageways to see the stalactites and other fascinating rock formations. Frequently they will stop to gaze at a particular Crinoidal fossil bed, or at a colourful band of rock crystal, locally known as Blue John. Little do they realise, while remarking at these natural wonders, they too are being studied by the Cavern Crawler. Lurking, out of sight in some shadowy recess, the monster listens to the familiar sounds as the party progresses, and tries to make sense of their unusual language.

Sometimes, when a child starts to cry, or when someone trips and falls, the Cavern Crawler immediately senses the distress and desperately wants to offer help or comfort. Unfortunately, the monster realises that it cannot approach for fear of causing a stampede, yet this strong affinity exists with the human visitors, and some inherent force compels it to be protective like a parent.

These interludes, close to the company of people are few and far between, and for much of the year the Cavern Crawler remains a solitary creature in its subterranean world. In the total darkness of the cave system, one day blends into the next, and each year passes without the changes of seasons. With endless time and few distractions the monster keeps busy in its natural playground.

Always restless and adventurous, the Cavern Crawler explores every possible passageway or opening no matter how awkward, in its relentless quest. Although quite a large and stocky monster, it has developed the ability to contort its body and squeeze into the most unlikely cracks. Its powerful arms and upper body aid climbing the steep cave walls as it searches out new routes through this hidden maze. Often the tunnels are narrow and low, making progress possible with a combination of crawling and snaking movements for considerable distances. Even these irritating problems present few barriers for the Cavern Crawler. It has no worries about time, and happily moves along using inbuilt navigational instincts to find its way around, even though the chosen route may take many hours or days.

The corrosive effect of underground water passing through limestone has produced many fascinating shapes in the rocks, making an ideal adventure playground for the Cavern Crawler. Always ready to stop and play when the opportunity arises, the monster frequently indulges in most ridiculous games, and is particularly fond of 'chimney drops'. This game starts with a strenuous climb up a vertical shaft, using its broad back to press against the smooth rock whilst inching upwards with hands and feet. This unusual activity only becomes exciting if great heights are ascended, then with deliberate decision, the Cavern Crawler relaxes and drops down the chimney, landing with a big splash in the deep pool below.

Once in the underground streams, the monster will play vigorously, sliding down the limestone chutes, showering under waterfalls and diving off the rocks into bottomless black pools. A change of activity is normally needed after these exhaustive hours of clambering around on the rocks, and a long relaxing swim begins in its favourite lake. This is a vast expanse of crystal clear water, perfectly still and tranquil beneath the lofty cavern roof. Only the Cavern Crawler and the fish that live there know of its existence, and the silence on entering this natural cathedral is infinite. Here the weary monster will push away from the side and glide out slowly and purposefully until somewhere out in the open water, its muscular arms gradually start to pull the creature forwards, in a fashion not dissimilar to our breast -stroke. This leisurely pursuit may continue in the darkness for several hours, with only the gentle lapping of water at the lake side to betray the monster's presence. Soon the urge for more energetic play will return, and with sudden impulse, the Cavern Crawler flips over onto its back. With arms and feet flailing the water into a foam, the monster rockets along the lake, snorting spray from its nostrils, and sending tidal waves against the limestone walls.

It is in the streams and passageways that the Cavern Crawler occasionally detects the presence of caver's, and with usual curiosity and concern, the monster abandons its activity to investigate the visitors. These unusual enthusiasts, clad in their special gear, have something in common with the Cavern Crawler, though certainly not in their appearance. A spirit of adventure drives them to attempt all manner of unthinkable feats of endurance. With bravery verging on insanity, the caver's will venture just as instinctively as the Cavern Crawler, through tiny cracks and holes so small that their chests need to be emptied of every last bit of air before they can squeeze through the rocks into the unknown. Their techniques have advanced to such a level that even the cold and foreboding depths of underground rivers and pools fail to deter the caver's of today, and it is in these dangerous situations that the Cavern Crawler keeps close by to ensure their safe return.

The monster becomes particularly worried when the caver's attempt to dive through a sump, where they may have to swim down through a flooded formation, rather like the u-bend of a toilet waste pipe, then hopefully come up to find air at the far side. The leading diver may receive a helpful push from behind as the monster directs directs him towards the safest exit, then some confusion may arise when he realises that no one else had started to follow. Sometimes it may be necessary for the Cavern Crawler to block up some of these underwater openings with rocks and boulders, in an attempt to avoid inevitable difficulties.

As the monster lay in its master den, contemplating its next activity, familiar noises from the show caves far to the north faintly echoed through the stone passageways, but these were distress signals of voices shouting and screaming. With immediate response the Cavern Crawler scrambled off in the direction of the disturbance, knowing that something was terribly wrong, and hoping that this time it could help.

Choosing the fastest routes to get to the scene as quickly as possible, the monster was soon in a position above the frantic group of people who were gathered around a deep hole at the far side of a barrier. The hysterical crying from a young family made it obvious to the Cavern Crawler that one of their children had fallen into the abyss. Knowing from its intimate knowledge, the monster realised that there would be little chance of surviving a fall down this particular hole, and desperately scrambled down a parallel shaft in search of the child.

The Cavern Crawler sobbed as it gently touched the crumpled body. With tender, slow deliberate movements, the monster picked up the child, and with one remaining hope, moved off in a purposeful manner.

The Peak District is famous for its limestone springs, some of which are believed to have special healing qualities. People for centuries have been prepared to travel great distances to bathe in these spring waters, especially at Buxton and Matlock where thriving towns have grown. Deep below ground the monster knew of another healing spring where water welled up inside a large cavern to form a shallow pond. The Cavern Crawler entered the chamber still gently carrying the limp child pressed against its massive chest, and with great care seated the infants battered frame in the pool so that its back leaned against the limestone wall.

The monster backed away as it tried to sense the overall layout of the cavern. Massive stalactites hung down from the roof and clusters of stalagmites pointed upwards from the cavern floor. These had formed over millions of years as rain water passed down through the rocks, then dripped from the cavern roof, leaving deposits of calcium carbonate carried in solution. The size of some of these stalactites, often several metres in length, gives some idea of the enormous time scale and stability of conditions for them to have matured. Some had grown to such an extent that the stalactites had joined up with the stalagmites to form solid pillars of rock, making progress difficult, even for the accomplished Cavern Crawler.

Derbyshire is also well known for its beautiful petrifying wells, where objects placed in them look as though they have been turned to stone. This again is due to the gradual process of lime deposition where tiny particles dissolved in the water are left behind as a thin coating on the objects.

Slowly, the monster waded across the shallow pool, as it had done so many times before. Seated around the edge were the 'petrified' bodies of other human casualties. The Cavern Crawler visited each in turn, gently touching their lime covered limbs to see if they had been healed by the mysterious water, but the stone-like bodies remained still and erect, in exactly the same position as they had been left by the monster. This macabre gathering of caver's and other visitors, all of whom had come to grief under ground, looked a pathetic sight as they sat silently in their limestone tomb. Only the steady gurgling of spring water upwelling into the pond disturbed the eternal peace.

No matter how careful the monster had been, and how admirable its intentions, the healing waters would never cure this unfortunate group of casualties, and now a child sits beside the others.

"A keen observer may notice the Alport Ape Man at rest on the precarious castle ledges."

CHAPTER
11
THE
ALPORT
APE
MAN

Numerous peaty streams flow southwards from Bleaklow,Hill. These in turn are joined by other streams as the River Alport begins its journey in a high moorland marsh, aptly named 'The Swamp'. The waters soon tumble down into a remote steep sided valley called Alport Dale where the river winds around across its narrow floor. This charming, peaceful valley, though close to the busy Snake Road, remains undisturbed by the hoards of tourists for most of the year, and even during the fine summer weekends, few people are to be seen off the beaten track.

The dale is dominated by the spectacular crags of Alport Castles. The hillside has slipped away at this famous geological site, leaving an enormous isolated stack of sandstone, high up near the moorland plateau. From most angles, Alport Castles makes an impressive sight with its great blocks towering majestically against the skyline like a fortress. The human eye has difficulty taking in the subtleties of this complex rock formation at first glance. Indeed, a complete circumnavigation of this awesome landmark is necessary before a full understanding of its immensity can be appreciated.

A keen observer may notice the Alport Ape Man at rest on the precarious castle ledges where it spends most of its time enjoying a thoroughly lazy lifestyle. From its lofty home, this intelligent monster looks out across the valley with panoramic vision, rather like a sentry, guarding the approach routes to its domain. Most visitors enter the valley from the south along a narrow farm road, and their every movement is closely scrutinised by the monster. This level of alertness does vary throughout the day however, for many hours are spent snoozing or day dreaming, especially when the sun is shining, or when the clouds passing overhead are just too fascinating for the Ape Man to look elsewhere.

Alport 'Castles' is appropriately named, for its vertical walls make an impenetrable fort. Its remoteness and inaccessibility have aided the preservation of this magnificent creature into the twentieth century with little interference from its human cousins. Only the hardy whitefaced sheep come near to the Alport Ape Man, as they graze unconcerned beneath its pedestal. The kestrel and jackdaw also occupy the same ledges, where they nest without fear of being disturbed.

These rocks are out of bounds to climbers and hikers who fortunately are guided by fences and footpaths around the outer edges of Alport Castles. This necessary management, not only protects the vulnerable landscape from erosion, but also helps to secure the monster's habitat.

A damp, chilly wind swirled around the Castles as the Alport Ape Man awoke. These inhospitable conditions do not worry this robust creature, for its thick covering of body hair allow it to withstand even the most severe winter extremes. This particular November morning may be depressing enough to deter any normal warm blooded animal, but for this monster, the day had special meaning. As it slowly stretched its massive limbs, the Ape Man remembered its plans, and began to clamber down the slippery rocks with more urgency than usual, causing it to slip and land with a thud on its bottom. Muttering under its breath, and rubbing its wounded parts, the creature persevered down the slope, more cautiously, towards the pool at the foot of the Castles.

The wind gusted strongly and whipped up little foaming waves on the water's surface. Undeterred, the monster waded in for its early morning bathe, and groomed itself enthusiastically from head to foot in preparation for an encounter with another creature that resides not very far away.

Some days ago when the weather had been clear, the Alport Ape Man had looked northwards from its castle, to the rugged skyline of Bleaklow Hill. The monster's keen eyes had spotted the familiar figure of the Bleaklow Bog Bouncer, silhouetted on the rocky horizon. With arms held high above their heads, a signal was made for the meeting of these two indefatigable individuals. On premeditated occasions, once a year, their paths cross. The Bleaklow Bog Bouncer travels towards the southern limit of its territory, and the Alport Ape Man climbs northwards, away from its fortress to a neutral site in the upper reaches of the Alport Valley.

Moving erect and purposefully through the mist, the Alport Ape Man traversed the steep grassy slopes as it aimed silently towards its rendezvous. Soon the tussocky grass changed to a thick blanket of golden bracken as the slope steepened towards the river. Confidently the monster moved downhill, splashed through the River Alport as though it did not exist, then, with arms swinging vigorously, it chose a diagonal route of ascent into the hills.

Now, standing high up on the valley side in a great natural amphitheatre, the Alport

Ape Man waited expectantly. The hill cloud began to clear from this vast arena, though the higher slopes overlooking the monster remained dark and obscure. This powerful hulk of a creature appeared almost dwarfed by the scale of its surroundings.

A sudden movement on the steep back wall, caught the monster's eye, but with cloud still swirling, there was no way to be sure that anything approached. The Alport Ape Man did not have to wait much longer, for out of the gloom bounding at reckless pace emerged the Bleaklow Bog Bouncer.

This energetic creature from the high moor, bounded to a halt in front of the Alport Ape Man. The monsters looked each other over as two evenly matched opponents tend to do before they battle. This special occasion was the annual wrestling contest between the superior strength of the Alport Ape Man, and the agility of the much smaller Bog Bouncer. Such a prestigious tournament as this would presumably attract a capacity audience, with supporters enough to fill a stadium, yet here they stood, on a perfect hillside setting, with only a few moorland sheep, and the odd red grouse to bear witness.

The Alport Ape Man was the first to move. Its nervous energy had coiled the monster like a steel spring, as it exploded with hands outstretched towards the relaxed and vulnerable Bog Bouncer. If the Ape Man had made contact, it would surely have crushed the slightly built contender, but with perfect timing, the Bog Bouncer side stepped and tripped the on-coming monster. Sprawling headlong through the grass on its chest, the Ape Man was temporarily unable to defend itself. This situation did not go unnoticed, for while it glided to a halt, the opportunist Bog Bouncer leapt repeatedly onto the Ape Man's exposed back.

The first round had undoubtedly been won by the cunning and confident Bog Bouncer, but this early mistake had jolted the Ape Man into a state of total readiness. Still feeling exhilarated by its initial success, the Bog Bouncer attempted another of its favourite trick moves. At first it lunged towards the Ape Man's ankles, seemingly attempting to topple this hairy giant, then with unexpected change of direction, the Bog Bouncer sprang high into the air with muscular legs ready to clamp the Ape Man's neck in a scissor move. Anticipating some sort of devious attack, the wily Ape Man was prepared, and grabbed the flying creature firmly with its great leathery hands. Like an Olympic hammer thrower, the Ape Man rotated and launched the squirming Bog Bouncer into the clouds. Fortunately landing on a springy bed of bracken, the Bog Bouncer sat up and felt for any broken bones before advancing once more.

This fascinating contest continued with furious pace throughout the blustery November afternoon. Both monsters were determined to win, as they were well aware of the prize at the end of the day. The red grouse had moved away to a safe distance where they spectated from a prominent rock, and a mountain hare sat transfixed on the hill top, looking down in disbelief at the maniacal creatures.

As usual, the battle was closely fought, with neither fighter gaining a clear advantage, until late in the day when night clouds were gathering in, the Alport Ape Man scored a series of points over the rapidly tiring Bog Bouncer, to achieve a decisive victory.

The monsters hugged and congratulated each other, then turned to leave the flattened hillside for another year. The two battered creatures were close to exhaustion, but the thought of their liquid prize kept them going as they hobbled over the hills together. A tradition had developed over the years for their celebration routine. The loser would accompany the winner to a nearby tavern, and treat the thirsty champion to as much ale as could be swallowed. Of course, the loser would also be sure to satisfy its own considerable capacity for the locally brewed liquor.

Side by side the two monsters sat in the cozy ale house, drinking glass after glass of the irresistible golden beer. The local customers were well used to this extraordinary event, and took little notice of this high spirited pair, but as the evening wore on, the monsters grew more and more inebriated, and their conversation became louder and boisterous. Eventually, the landlord concerned for the reputation of his tavern, firmly suggested that it was time for them to leave.

A cold, wet blast of air entered the bar room as the Bleaklow Bog Bouncer held the door open for his comrade, who was finding some difficulty in-coordinating his movements. A fierce storm had built up while they had been enjoying themselves indoors, and heavy rain lashed at the monsters as they helped each other along the pavement. Across the street, a welcoming glow and familiar smell attracted them like a magnet. The village fish and chip shop was still open. Joining on the end of the queue, the monsters waited patiently for their turn to be served, and wasted no time in devouring their enormous portions. The evening would not have been complete without this hearty supper, and so, with appetites satisfied, and eye lids drooping, they went on their separate ways into the hills.

Alport Castles looked black and formidable against the stormy night sky as the Ape Man scrambled up to its home. Terrifying claps of thunder resounded through the valley, and flashes of lightening threatened to shatter the monster's sandstone tower. At last, the creature stood on the highest pinnacle as the wind howled around its feet, and with defiant gesture to the storm, the Ape Man began to beat its massive chest. A heavy rhythmical beat boomed louder and louder, until at last, even the tumultuous sky relinquished its power to the guardian of Alport Dale.

"In familiar posture, the Kinder Cruncher sat with its broad back against a large gritstone tor, contentedly crunching a rock between powerful hands."

CHAPTER
12
THE
KINDER
CRUNCHER

Christmas Eve on Kinder looked like a picture postcard, with the winter sun shining on the snowdrifts, and ice crystals sparkling on the rocks where arctic conditions had established. In familiar posture, the Kinder Cruncher sat with its broad back against a large gritstone tor, contentedly crunching a rock between powerful hands. Snow had filled in all the hollows and gaps on the plateau surface, though isolated rocky outcrops remained exposed to the biting wind. During the day the monster would typically spend many hours in the same position, working away at a rock, and creating a deep pile of debris and sand in the process.

On this particular day, the Cruncher had purposefully chosen a barren wilderness site called Ringing Roger. At this time of year, the monster did not expect to be disturbed too much by people, even though this rocky hill top is within easy walking distance from the popular village of Edale. A lone hiker did come very close however, but there was no reason for concern, as the Cruncher in its calm sort of way, simply moved around the gritstone outcrop where it was working, keeping low and out of the line of vision. The hiker stood within touching distance of the monster for several minutes as he studied his map and looked across the snow covered Grindsbrook valley, unaware of his company.

Soon, the Cruncher was alone once more, and able to continue the laborious task it had started earlier in the day. The monster was in the final stages of making a set of rounded rocks which would be used later for playing a game, very similar to boules. The aim of this addictive game, is to throw the heavy stones so that they land as close as possible to a smaller 'jack' stone. Over the years, a vast area of rock fragments, pebbles and sand, has taken the place of moorland heather, and even the thick layer of peaty soil has been lost due to this obsessive activity. The loose bed of gritstone particles at Ringing Roger now makes an ideal site for the game, as the rocks can land in the soft material without rolling away. The monster has acquired considerable skill with its throwing hand, and is capable of lobbing a stone with amazing accuracy.

Occasionally and quite unexpectedly, the Cruncher will be joined by its neighbouring monsters, the Glossop Gliders. These migratory creatures sometimes look down on the Kinder Cruncher as it practices alone on the high moorland plateau. The Gliders have changed the rules of the game to suit their physical differences, and usually make a good match for the experienced Cruncher. Having large wings, more suited to covering great distances, the Gliders have some trouble coming in low to drop their rocks. They will pick up a single rock in flight with one grasping foot; then regain some height, taking several large circles to do this. Only when the Glider is completely satisfied with its line of approach, will it open its fleshy toes to release the stone into the game area. Normally each member of the flock will insist on a turn, however, the dominant Glider as might be expected, takes more than its fair share of drops. As with most activities, the Glossop Gliders keep up their continuous racket while the game is in progress, then without formality they will depart, leaving the Kinder Cruncher in peace once more.

At night, the monster becomes more active and industrious, being nocturnal by nature. Although its excessive body weight restricts movement, it normally travels several kilometres along Kinder's edges, under cover of darkness. The Kinder Cruncher will work at one of its gritstone sculptures for several hours at a time, rasping away with its broad hands to create magnificent works of art, not dissimilar to Henry Moore's creations.

The monster's sculptures can be seen at numerous sites around the plateau's rocky edges, but the most notable locations are at 'Seal Stones' and 'Fairbrook Naze' on the northern side of Kinder, and at the 'Wool Packs' to the south. The latter example is by far the most dramatic, with dozens of isolated shapes grouped amongst the heather, like living things. The sizes vary from just the height of a person, to the immensity of a house with all the corners carefully rounded and shaped to the exacting design of the Kinder Cruncher. The shapes are diverse and beautiful, with a hint of practicality, for some have been made into tables, chairs, mushrooms, anvils and creatures of various sorts. Faces have also been fashioned in gritstone, especially at the craggy edges where nose-like profiles can be seen in proliferation. The monster deserves some merit for these achievements, as many faces have been sculpted in exposed positions where considerable courage and determination must have been needed.

Few people really appreciate the Kinder Cruncher's work, and geographers or scientists would give a completely different explanation for the existence of these weird gritstone shapes. They are likely to dismiss the unproven possibility of a monster with such creative ability. Their theory would point to other forces at work, such as wind and temperature change. Textbooks will have shown them how water expands when it gets into cracks in the rocks and freezes, thus breaking off pieces of gritstone. People who are unconvinced about the monster's existence may need to get wrapped up in warm clothing and hope they will be lucky enough to witness the sculptor at work, preferably on a mild moon lit night. Such an expedition as this is really for the experienced hill walker, and certainly not for the feint hearted.

The evening sky had now settled over Kinder, and a multitude of stars twinkled as far as the eye could see. A bright moon illuminated the moor and reflected on patches of snow where it clung to the heather. The temperature had dropped several more degrees below freezing point, making this barren wilderness a hostile place without exaggeration.

In the cozy security of the Edale valley, children hung up their Christmas stockings, and families throughout the District followed their familiar routines and traditions. A warm light shone from each home, and a comforting smell of burning wood drifted in the winter sky.

High on the moor, the Kinder Cruncher eagerly awaited the arrival of other Crunchers as they slowly homed in on the Ringing Roger site. Christmas Eve was also a time for these normally solitary monsters to re-establish their family links, and relatives of various ages and sizes gradually gathered from all corners of the plateau. The Kinder population would soon be complete, being modest in numbers, yet strong in spirit. Together, their games had special meaning, and now, their year long practise at throwing the stones would be put to the test as the Kinder Cruncher proudly displayed its new set. Bitterly cold as it was, the Crunchers played enthusiastically, long into the night. Only after many captivating games did the Crunchers reluctantly depart. Each match guaranteed total concentration from players and spectators alike. Some had scrambled up onto their gritstone seats for a better view, and the moon had been kind enough to provide floodlighting for their gathering. In the early hours of Christmas morning, the contented monsters happily set out along the well worn tracks, each heading for its own hill top home.

The satisfied Kinder Cruncher sat on its favourite rock as it watched the last of its relatives disappear into the darkness. The night's activity had churned up every inch of the ground , making it look more like a race track, but soon the winter weather would hide every trace of their prints.

Some observant readers may have noticed a strong similarity between Kinder's stony waste sites and other hill top places around the British Isles. Perhaps other Cruncher clans would also be gathered in their own remote locations, peacefully engaged in their unique activities.

If anyone is fortunate enough to come across a Cruncher while walking in the hills, please give it plenty of space, and take some time to appreciate its ways.

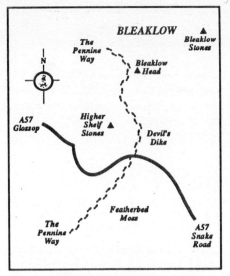

Monster's habitat.

THE BLEAKLOW BOG BOUNCER

General Description:

This lively creature is extremely well adapted to its environment. Its long legs and large feet allow it to make amazing leaps from tussock to tussock, across the boggy Bleaklow terrain. The Bog Bouncer is capable of changing colour, to avoid detection throughout the seasons of the year.

Haunt:

Restricted mainly to the Bleaklow upland, with occasional visits to Kinder Scout a few kilometres to the south.

Habits:
As with most Peak District monsters the Bleaklow Bog Bouncer is very secretive and is rarely seen during the day. It enjoys bouncing at sunrise and at sunset, when its silhouette can sometimes be seen on the horizon.

Den:

Several dens may be used on the Bleaklow plateau. These are normally sheltered natural hollows among the gritstone tors, offering good visibility in most directions.

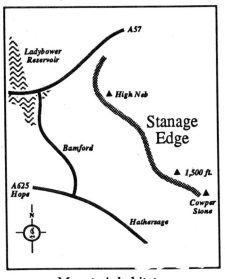

Monster's habitat.

THE STANAGE STOMPER

General Description:

The Stanage Stomper is a heavy and ungainly monster. It is always very grumpy, and spends much of its time stomping along Stanage Edge on its one thick leg. The large footprint can easily be recognised in the snow.

Haunt:

The well trodden path along Stanage Edge provides an excellent stomping ground, being firm underfoot and mainly level.

Habits:

The Stanage Stomper tends to be particularly active at dusk after the climbers and ramblers have gone. In between active periods, it may spend hours standing motionless disguised as a rock.

Den:

Due to its tough skin and well camouflaged appearance, the Stanage Stomper rarely needs any shelter, preferring to stay outside in all weathers.

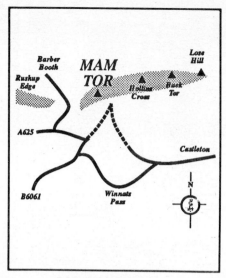

Monster's habitat.

THE MAM TOR MUMMY

General Description:

This is the tallest of all the Peak District Monsters, standing nearly 4 metres in height. Its body is covered in white bandage from head to foot, making its movements awkward but surprisingly fast.

Haunt:

The Mummy walks the rounded grassy summit of Mam Tor, moving silently and swiftly, as though in pursuit of some unseen being.

Habits:

Month after month may pass without anything unusual on the hill, then without warning, The Mummy will appear out of the mist. Its presence may cause a few heads to turn in disbelief before it passes out of sight.

Den:

Little is known about the Mummy's hiding place, but legend says that a labyrinth of hidden passageways exists below the surface of Mam Tor, leading to long forgotten burial chambers.

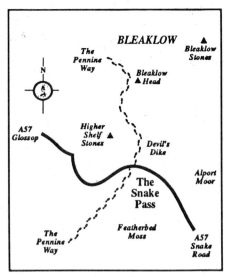

Monster's habitat.

THE SNAKE PASS SLIME SLITHERER

General Description:

This slimy, repulsive thing is most active in spring, when the ditches and groughs are full of melt water, and the dark peat bogs are overflowing. The Slitherer has developed webbed fingers and toes, which help it move rapidly through the quagmire.

Haunt:

The main road between Sheffield and Glossop passes over a wild moorland area called Snake Pass. This territory belongs to the Slime Slitherer. Only the most observant traveller will see this elusive creature. as it stealthily moves around the southern Bleaklow slopes and Featherbed Moss.

Habits:

A favourite pastime of the Slime Slitherer, is to pull itself up to the top of a deep peat grough, and toboggan down on its belly, using its webbed hands for propulsion. It frequently has to cross the busy Snake Road in search of suitable slithering grounds. These are very anxious moments, as the tarmac surface presents obvious problems for this amphibious creature.

Den:

The Slime Slitherer pushes itself deep into the side of a peat grough towards the end of May. Here it hibernates through the drier summer months, and emerges in October, refreshed after its long rest.

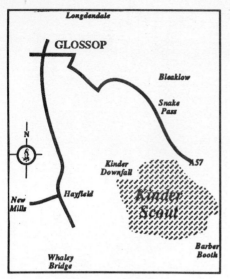

Monster's habitat.

THE GLOSSOP GLIDER

General Description:

Unlike other Peak District monsters, which are mainly solitary, the Glossop Glider tends to appear in small flocks, often soaring high in the sky over the western hill slopes. Although its body is no more than two metres in length, it has a wing span in excess of six metres.

Haunt:

Sightings of the Glossop Glider have been recorded as far away as the Cuillin Mountains of Skye, to the north, and the Trent Lowlands, to the south east. Its seasonal haunt encompasses the hills around Glossop in the summer months, but little is known of its migration routes during the rest of the year.

Habits:

The Glossop Glider soars so high in the sky that it can normally only be seen as a speck, as it takes advantage of rising thermals. Several hang gliders have recently noticed these monsters, circling high above them near Rushup Edge.

Den:

At night, the flocks come down to roost on high rocky ledges, where they screech and squawk to each other, above the noise of the wind. The crags around Kinder Downfall are considered to be their predominant roost.

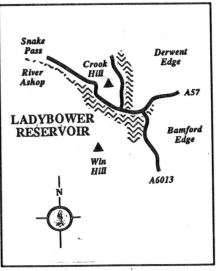

Monster's habitat.

THE LADYBOWER LURKER

General Description:

Very few people have encountered the Ladybower Lurker. Some fly fishermen have noticed the playful behaviour of this freshwater mammal, which breathes through a short snorkel-like trunk. Its bulging eyes, set near the top of its head, can swivel round through 360 degrees, just above the surface of the water.

Haunt:

The Lurker enjoys the unrestricted stretches of open water between Derwent Dam, to the north, and Ladybower Dam, to the south. During periods of heavy floodwater, it may travel as far upstream as Hagg Farm Hostel, which is sited close to the River Ashop.

Habits:

The Ladybower Lurker loves to swim at high speed along the long reservoir channels, causing a noticeable wake on the surface of the water. Sometimes it will play hide and seek with fly fishermen in their rowing boats or near the waters edge.

Den:

Beneath the surface of Ladybower Reservoir lie abandoned houses, now forgotten and out of sight. These are now the adopted homes of the Ladybower Lurker.

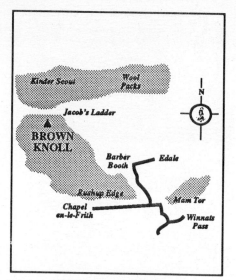

Monster's habitat.

THE BROWN KNOLL BEAUTY

General Description:

From a distance, this creature may resemble a beautiful dark haired maiden, with long flowing hair, and slim shapely figure. On closer inspection, her face is so ugly, that anyone unfortunate enough to meet her will collapse from shock, or lose control of their senses.

Haunt:

Between Kinder Scout and Mam Tor, lies a windswept ridge, dominated by Brown Knoll. Here, in the grassy tussocks, sits the monster, known as the Brown Knoll Beauty.

Habits:

She will often entice the unsuspecting male hiker or fellrunner, away from the track, with her inviting appearance. Only when the victim is at close range, will she turn her ugly face, and laugh hysterically in great amusement.

Den:

During the summer months, the Brown Knoll Beauty prefers to stay out on the hill, but as the nights become cooler, she finds shelter in derelict stone barns.

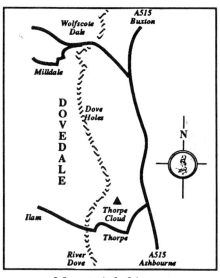

Monster's habitat.

THE DOVEDALE DEAD HEAD

General Description:

The Dovedale Dead Head frequently stumbles along the main tourist path, with shoulders slumped forwards and arms hanging limp. Rotten flesh hangs from its grisly head. Maggots swarm inside its mouth, and worms slither from its eye sockets.

Haunt:

Only the easy paths next to the River Dove are suitable for this wretched creature. It remains trapped in its steep walled prison, where it must wander through time.

Habits:

Visitors may pass by the Dovedale Dead Head, without really noticing that something is terribly wrong. It wears a full length hooded anorak, which normally hides its hideous face.

Den:

There are many cave entrances in the limestone walls along Dovedale. These provide some seclusion, especially during the busy summer days.

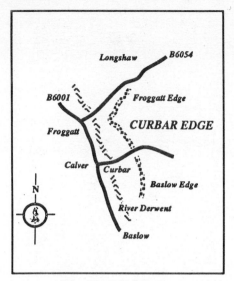

Monster's habitat.

THE CURBAR CLAMBERER

General Description:

Most rock climbers would be very envious of the Curbar Clamberer, if they had the chance to witness its amazing acrobatic manoeuvres. It is equipped with long muscular arms, thick grasping fingers and toes, and overdeveloped teeth for holding onto rocks.

Haunt:

The Gritstone edges overlooking the River Derwent, are ideal for this small but agile monster. It feels most at home on the rocks of Curbar Edge, but frequent visits are made to crags to the north and south.

Habits:

The Curbar Clamberer is accustomed to large numbers of climbers and ramblers inside its territory, but makes no attempt to hide away. This amiable little monster clambers around unnoticed and undeterred. Its favourite technique is to climb overhanging sections, by holding firmly onto the rock with its teeth, whilst moving its legs through 180 degrees over the overhang.

Den:

The Curbar Clamberer shares its den with the jackdaws and doves, deep inside the cracks of Curbar Edge.

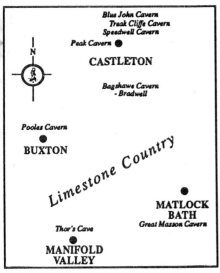

Monster's habitat.

THE CAVERN CRAWLER

General Description:

Most creatures which live in the total darkness of subterranean caverns, have evolved a lifestyle to suit their mysterious surroundings. The Cavern Crawler is no exception. With no need for eyes, it now relies on its well developed senses of hearing, smelling and touching.

Haunt:

The Cavern Crawler is capable of travelling incredible distances along the natural tunnels and underground streams. Unknown passageways through the limestone, link the Castleton area to the Manifold Valley in the south.

Habits:

With endless time, and few distractions, the Cavern Crawler keeps busy in its natural playground. It climbs, swims, dives and crawls, along the silent pathways. Only when the show caverns open their doors to the tourists, does the Cavern Crawler stop and listen. These are moments of great excitement for the monster, and well worth a long crawl to its secret vantage points.

Den:

The Cavern Crawlers favourite den is a small chamber with tunnels leading off in several directions. From this strategic point, the monster can quickly scurry along to any part of Derbyshire's limestone country.

71

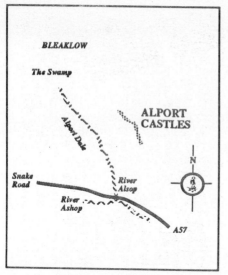

Monster's habitat.

THE ALPORT APE MAN

General Description:

This magnificent creature has survived into the twentieth century with little interference from its human cousins. A thick covering of body hair has protected this monster through the severe Pennine winters. Its powerful limbs help it to move easily around Alport Dales spectacular rocky crags.

Haunt:

The Alport Apeman prefers a lazy life, sitting around on the abundant gritstone ledges and outcrops in Alport Dale. Recently, the forested slopes in the region have become mature enough to provide useful cover, during times of intense tourist invasion.

Habits:

When the wind and sleet lash the rugged hillsides, lesser humans seek shelter in the valleys. Only the Alport Apeman welcomes these storms. The monster climbs to the highest rock and stands beating its massive chest in defiance.

Den:

High rocky ledges which face into the midday sun, are preferred during periods of settled weather. Hollows in the grassy hillside are also frequently used throughout the year.

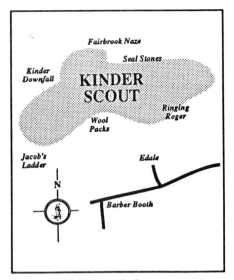

Monster's habitat.

THE KINDER CRUNCHER

General Description:

This rather overweight and slothful monster peacefully exists high up on the Kinder plateau. Thick layers of body fat keep it warm through the icy winter nights. The Kinder Cruncher is rarely seen during the day. Being nocturnal, it tends to move around slowly through the heather and rocks, under the cover of darkness.

Haunt:

Kinder Scouts varied and extensive terrain provides the perfect habitat for this contented monster. Although capable of spending long periods of time sitting in snow drifts and deep heather, it prefers to live amongst the gritstone tors.

Habits:

The monster's name is derived from its unusual pastime of breaking stones with its powerful grip. The Kinder Cruncher often starts the day with a sizeable piece of gritstone, which it systematically breaks down,into pebbles and sand. This habit is so ingrained, that stones are frequently carried from the edges to the heathery central regions, for the purpose mentioned above.

Den:

Like its neighbour (The Bleaklow Bog Bouncer), the Kinder Cruncher finds shelter near the gritstones. Even during busy summer days, the monster remains undetected by moving around the stones, always keeping low and out of vision.

"from footprint to finished book"

CIRCULAR WALK GUIDES -

SHORT CIRCULAR WALKS IN THE PEAK DISTRICT - Vol. 1 and 2
CIRCULAR WALKS IN WESTERN PEAKLAND
SHORT CIRCULAR WALKS IN THE STAFFORDSHIRE MOORLANDS
SHORT CIRCULAR WALKS - TOWNS & VILLAGES OF THE PEAK DISTRICT
SHORT CIRCULAR WALKS AROUND MATLOCK
SHORT CIRCULAR WALKS IN THE DUKERIES
SHORT CIRCULAR WALKS IN SOUTH YORKSHIRE
SHORT CIRCULAR WALKS IN SOUTH DERBYSHIRE
SHORT CIRCULAR WALKS AROUND BUXTON
SHORT CIRCULAR WALKS AROUND WIRKSWORTH
SHORT CIRCULAR WALKS IN THE HOPE VALLEY
40 SHORT CIRCULAR WALKS IN THE PEAK DISTRICT
CIRCULAR WALKS ON KINDER & BLEAKLOW
SHORT CIRCULAR WALKS IN SOUTH NOTTINGHAMSHIRE
SHIRT CIRCULAR WALKS IN CHESHIRE
SHORT CIRCULAR WALKS IN WEST YORKSHIRE
CIRCULAR WALKS TO PEAK DISTRICT AIRCRAFT WRECKS by John Mason
CIRCULAR WALKS IN THE DERBYSHIRE DALES
SHORT CIRCULAR WALKS IN EAST DEVON
SHORT CIRCULAR WALKS AROUND HARROGATE
SHORT CIRCULAR WALKS IN CHARNWOOD FOREST
SHORT CIRCULAR WALKS AROUND CHESTERFIELD
SHORT CIRCULAR WALKS IN THE YORKS DALES - Vol 1 - Southern area.
SHORT CIRCULAR WALKS IN THE AMBER VALLEY (Derbyshire)
SHORT CIRCULAR WALKS IN THE LAKE DISTRICT
SHORT CIRCULAR WALKS IN THE NORTH YORKSHIRE MOORS
SHORT CIRCULAR WALKS IN EAST STAFFORDSHIRE
DRIVING TO WALK - 16 Short Circular walks south of London by Dr. Simon Archer
LONG CIRCULAR WALKS IN THE PEAK DISTRICT - Vol.1 2 and 3.
LONG CIRCULAR WALKS IN THE STAFFORDSHIRE MOORLANDS
LONG CIRCULAR WALKS IN CHESHIRE
WALKING THE TISSINGTON TRAIL
WALKING THE HIGH PEAK TRAIL
WALKING THE MONSAL TRAIL & OTHER DERBYSHIRE TRAILS

CANAL WALKS -

VOL 1 - DERBYSHIRE & NOTTINGHAMSHIRE
VOL 2 - CHESHIRE & STAFFORDSHIRE
VOL 3 - STAFFORDSHIRE
VOL 4 - THE CHESHIRE RING
VOL 5 - LINCOLNSHIRE & NOTTINGHAMSHIRE
VOL 6 - SOUTH YORKSHIRE
VOL 7 - THE TRENT & MERSEY CANAL

JOHN MERRILL DAY CHALLENGE WALKS -

WHITE PEAK CHALLENGE WALK
DARK PEAK CHALLENGE WALK
PEAK DISTRICT END TO END WALKS
STAFFORDSHIRE MOORLANDS CHALLENGE WALK
THE LITTLE JOHN CHALLENGE WALK

74

YORKSHIRE DALES CHALLENGE WALK
NORTH YORKSHIRE MOORS CHALLENGE WALK
LAKELAND CHALLENGE WALK
THE RUTLAND WATER CHALLENGE WALK
MALVERN HILLS CHALLENGE WALK
THE SALTER'S WAY
THE SNOWDON CHALLENGE
CHARNWOOD FOREST CHALLENGE WALK
THREE COUNTIES CHALLENGE WALK (Peak District).
CAL-DER-WENT WALK by Geoffrey Carr,
THE QUANTOCK WAY
BELVOIR WITCHES CHALLENGE WALK

INSTRUCTION & RECORD -
HIKE TO BE FIT.....STROLLING WITH JOHN
THE JOHN MERRILL WALK RECORD BOOK

MULTIPLE DAY WALKS -
THE RIVERS'S WAY
PEAK DISTRICT: HIGH LEVEL ROUTE
PEAK DISTRICT MARATHONS
THE LIMEY WAY
THE PEAKLAND WAY

COAST WALKS & NATIONAL TRAILS -
ISLE OF WIGHT COAST PATH
PEMBROKESHIRE COAST PATH
THE CLEVELAND WAY
WALKING ANGELSEY'S COASTLINE.

CYCLING Compiled by Arnold Robinson.
CYCLING AROUND THE NORTH YORK MOORS
CYCLING AROUND CASTLETON & the Hope Valley.

PEAK DISTRICT HISTORICAL GUIDES -
A to Z GUIDE OF THE PEAK DISTRICT
DERBYSHIRE INNS - an A to Z guide
HALLS AND CASTLES OF THE PEAK DISTRICT & DERBYSHIRE
TOURING THE PEAK DISTRICT & DERBYSHIRE BY CAR
DERBYSHIRE FOLKLORE
PUNISHMENT IN DERBYSHIRE
CUSTOMS OF THE PEAK DISTRICT & DERBYSHIRE
WINSTER - a souvenir guide
ARKWRIGHT OF CROMFORD
LEGENDS OF DERBYSHIRE
DERBYSHIRE FACTS & RECORDS
TALES FROM THE MINES by Geoffrey Carr
PEAK DISTRICT PLACE NAMES by Martin Spray

JOHN MERRILL'S MAJOR WALKS -
TURN RIGHT AT LAND'S END
WITH MUSTARD ON MY BACK
TURN RIGHT AT DEATH VALLEY
EMERALD COAST WALK

SKETCH BOOKS -
SKETCHES OF THE PEAK DISTRICT

COLOUR BOOK:-
THE PEAK DISTRICT.......something to remember her by.

OVERSEAS GUIDES -
HIKING IN NEW MEXICO - Vol I - The Sandia and Manzano Mountains.
Vol 2 - Hiking "Billy the Kid" Country. Vol 4 - N.W. area - " Hiking Indian Country."
"WALKING IN DRACULA COUNTRY" - Romania.

VISITOR GUIDES -
MATLOCK . BAKEWELL. ASHBOURNE.